Starcat's Corner:

Essays on Pagan Living

Starcat's Corner:

Essays on Pagan Living

N. Starcat Shields

MOON
BOOKS

Winchester, UK
Washington, USA

First published by Moon Books, 2013
Moon Books is an imprint of John Hunt Publishing Ltd., Laurel House, Station Approach,
Alresford, Hants, SO24 9JH, UK
office1@jhpbooks.net
www.johnhuntpublishing.com
www.moon-books.net

For distributor details and how to order please visit the 'Ordering' section on our website.

Text copyright: N. Starcat Shields 2012

ISBN: 978 1 78099 553 3

Design: Stuart Davies

Printed and bound in the USA by Edwards Brothers Malloy

We operate a distinctive and ethical publishing philosophy in all
areas of our business, from our global network of authors to
production and worldwide distribution.

CONTENTS

Preface   1

Chapter 1: Samhain   **5**
Samhain 1997: House Cleansing   6
Samhain 1998: Pagan Parenting   7
Samhain 1999: Samhain and Popular Culture   9
Samhain 2000: The Dark Mother   11
Samhain 2002: Touching the Gods   12
Samhain 2003: Pagan Homeschooling   14
Samhain 2004: A Turning Point   15
Samhain 2005: In Defense of Optimism   17
Samhain 2006: Touching the Ancestors   19
Samhain 2007: Positive Magick   21
Samhain 2008: A Mindful Retreat   23

Chapter 2: Yule   **26**
Yule 1997: A Quieter Holiday Season   27
Yule 1998: Saturnalia Dream   29
Yule 1999: Turning Inward: How to Get Through
   the Dark Time of Year   30
Yule 2000: Gifts for Yourself   32
Yule 2001: Blessings of Community   34
Yule 2002: A Solstice Tale   36
Yule 2003: Book of Shadows   38
Yule 2005: What Do You Mean, 'Pagan Lent?'   40
Yule 2006: Emotions and Change   42
Yule 2007: Self in Community   43
Yule 2008: Finding Magick Everywhere   46

Chapter 3: Imbolc   **48**
Imbolc 1997: Journeys to Create Reality: Walking   49

Imbolc 1998: Ice Storms   50
Imbolc 2000: Wicca and Astrology: A Book Review   52
Imbolc 2001: Patterns   54
Imbolc 2002: Listening   56
Imbolc 2003: Beneath the Surface   57
Imbolc 2004: Healing in a Crisis   61
Imbolc 2006: Paying Attention   63
Imbolc 2007: Unlocking Your Faerie Senses   65
Imbolc 2008: President Who?   68
Imbolc 2009: A Simpler Way   70

Chapter 4: Ostara   **73**
Ostara 1997: Journeys to Create Reality: The Road Trip   74
Ostara 2000: Reclaiming Faith   75
Ostara 2001: Magickal Stories   77
My Friend Blacky   77
The World of Books   78
Remembering the Magick   79
Ostara 2002: Rain, Rain   80
Ostara 2004: Non-Attachment   82
Ostara 2005: Seeking Balance   84
Ostara 2006: Tending the Spiritual Garden   86
Ostara 2007: Spring Cleansing   88
Ostara 2009: Paganism in the New Age   90

Chapter 5: Beltane   **95**
Beltane 1997: City Witch   96
Beltane 1998: A Radical Notion   98
Beltane 2000: Alternative Religions' Night Out   99
Beltane 2001: Inner Male and Female   102
Beltane 2002: We Are the Earth   104
Beltane 2003: Perfect Love and Perfect Trust   106
Beltane 2005: Beyond Self-Doubt   108
Beltane 2006: Tending the Temple   110

Beltane 2007: Joyful Intentions   113
Beltane 2008: Navigating the Seas of Change   115

Chapter 6: Litha   **118**
Litha 1997: Mazzim   119
Litha 1998: Making a Living   120
Litha 2000: Letting Go   121
Litha 2001: Silence   123
Litha 2002: Light My Fire   124
Litha 2003: It Really *Is* a Temple   126
Litha 2005: Pagan Summer Fun   128
Litha 2006: Faeries, Flowers and Fun   129
Litha 2007: The Upward Spiral   131
Litha 2008: Creating a Living   133

Chapter 7: Lammas   **136**
Lammas 1997: Memory   137
Lammas 1999: Journals   138
Lammas 2000: Where Does the Time Go?   140
Lammas 2001: The Bridge of Ambiguity   142
Lammas 2002: Creatures of Air   143
Lammas 2003: Are You an 'HSP?'   146
Lammas 2005: Healthy Communities   148
Lammas 2006: Barefoot Hiking   150
Lammas 2009: The Spiral of Spiritual Growth   151
Seeking   153
Contemplation   154
Practice   155
Awakening   157
Teaching   158

Chapter 8: Mabon   **160**
Mabon 1997: Pagans in the Community   161
Mabon 1999: Stepping Into the Priesstesshood   163

Mabon 2000: Symbols   164
Mabon 2001: The Flow of Creative Energy   166
Mabon 2002: A Quest for Balance   168
Mabon 2003: Keeping Your Balance   170
Mabon 2004: A Harvest of Creativity   172
Mabon 2007: Storing the Harvest   174
Mabon 2008: Choosing Love   175
Mabon 2009: Questions, Milestones and Pendulums   177

References   181

Dedication

To Quester, for always having faith in me, and for all the years of love and support.

To BlackLion, for being a loving and inspiring partner and believing the dream.

And to my parents, for giving me life and encouraging me to pursue my passions.

Preface

I stepped onto the wide wooden porch of the chalet, full of a bubbly mix of elation and nerves. I was here at last! I was about to step into the all-camp, opening night meeting of the 2005 Vermont Witch Camp. This was the retreat of my dreams: a whole week on a remote mountainside with 125 other Pagans, all focused on deepening our spiritual connection. Bliss!

That afternoon I'd driven up from Maine by myself, checked in and set up camp. The theme of the gathering centered on Lewis Carroll's *Alice in Wonderland*, and I truly felt like I was stepping through the looking glass into another world. Late-summer days stretched out ahead of me, sparkling with magick and potential.

During this first meeting, I listened carefully. Which of the learning paths should I choose to follow? What about an affinity group? And the extra offerings, like yoga classes and drumming workshops? I was immediately drawn to the path called 'Joining to Mystery.' The intention of the path's two teachers was to help us create sacred relationships with the unseen worlds and the spirits of nature.

One of the 'Joining to Mystery' teachers, Angela Magara, was a tall, confident priestess whose vibrant energy and long blond hair cascaded down around her like a cloak. She also planned to offer a writing intensive throughout the week. It appealed to me, but that first night I wrote in my journal that I'd decided not to take the writing track. I would already have Angela as a path teacher, and part of my intention for camp was to 'just be,' rather than focusing on 'trying to create some kind of finished writing project.'

The next morning, though, as my journal details, 'when I went to sit down at breakfast, I saw some women I'd met at dinner last night and happened thus upon the Ecstatic Writing

Group. I sat down and was immediately drawn in by what Angela was saying, so I've joined! It seems to feel right for me, after all.' Angela was direct and inspiring in her challenge. She told us, 'There are hundreds of books on how to be a Pagan or learn basic Wicca 101. What we need are writings by those who are out there living it. We need more books about the experience of being a Pagan. You have the gift of words, so share it.'

Over the course of the amazing and transformative week, I began to step into the roles I was creating for myself. My mantra was 'Writing, Dancing, Healing.' One of my vows as we prepared to take our new wisdom back into our communities was to, in Angela's words, 'spin the holy words out of myself.' I was determined to meet the challenge, even as I returned to my full-time job and parenting my young kids. The task seemed daunting, but I brought back with me a new commitment to a regular writing practice and the seeds of a deeper connection to my muse.

In fact, I was already writing regularly about my life as a Pagan. I'd been writing a column called *Starcat's Corner* in my local Pagan newsletter for nearly ten years. It had started with a letter to the EarthTides Pagan Network in 1997, as I tentatively reached out of my solitary witch status in search of community. Gradually I began sharing my own thoughts and experiences. As I grew more confident in my abilities, I offered tools and suggestions for readers who wished to enhance their personal spirituality and live in harmony with others and the planet.

When I returned from Vermont Witch Camp, excited about my new focus, my husband Quester suggested that I collect the *Starcat's Corner* essays into a book. It made a lot of sense. I could address the need Angela spoke about, which was essentially answering the question: 'How do you live your earth-based spirituality, day in and day out, particularly in a culture that doesn't share your values?'

In this book, I bring you one woman's answers, discovered over time. Having chosen a path less traveled, I offer it up in hopes that my experiences will encourage you in your own practice of the Craft. The ideas, tools and suggestions contained within these essays offer assistance in the search for meaning beneath the surface of the modern mainstream lifestyle. The focus is on finding a balanced connection to the earth, one that encompasses body, mind, emotions and spirit. And lest you think I speak from on high, Pagan living is an ongoing, day-by-day practice. As you'll see within these pages, we human beings are continually facing challenges, posing questions and seeking answers.

Why am I called to share these particular tools with you? In my experience over two decades of active Pagan living, there wasn't one particular teacher or tradition that fit me just perfectly. I've been an eclectic witch from the start, creating my own path piece by piece. And yet even as I've accumulated wisdom from many sources, I've noticed universal tools and practices that seem to fit well into any belief system. Over time, some of my own recurring patterns have also seemed to be common human challenges. I feel drawn to provide suggestions, to share what I've learned through trial and error. Part of my calling is to offer these solutions to you as you walk your own unique path, in hopes of helping you along the way, inspiring you to persevere and to thrive.

The essays are arranged by Sabbat. As we follow the Wheel of the Year, we align ourselves with the cycles of nature. Even in our modern civilized culture, we are mammals, part of the natural world. Our cycles of growth parallel those of the earth's other beings; the plants and birds, trees and animals. Within this context, we become attuned with the elements, ponder our purpose in life and continue to deepen our wisdom with each passing year. Some of the topics covered here include faith, creativity, releasing stress, overcoming self-doubt, dealing with change, mindfulness meditation, barefoot hiking, faeries, creating prosperity and more. Over time, my writing style has matured as my understanding continues to grow. You may notice the evolution of my ideas and practices as you read through the essays in each Sabbat. In the same way, each season brings particular themes of thought and action.

This book you hold represents a culmination of sorts, and also a beginning. In the years since Witch Camp, I've taken many steps towards living my dreams. In 2008, I left my full-time career to pursue my creativity and take my turn at homeschooling my two kids. It was a leap of faith and progress has seemed slow at times. Yet following my callings, like walking my Pagan path, is extremely rewarding. At last I have stepped into the author and teacher role I've been working towards for many years. I bring you these essays on Pagan living, in hope that the lessons I've been learning will provide you with hope and inspiration as you, too, reach toward your dreams.

N.S.S.

Chapter 1

Samhain

Samhain, observed on October 31, is also known as the Celtic New Year. The harvest season is ending, yet the Wheel of the Year continues to turn, heading towards the sun's rebirth at the Winter Solstice. We sow our hopes and wishes like winter crops. We ready ourselves for the cold season, releasing what is no longer needed and preparing our homes for harsher weather. It's time to dedicate ourselves to introspective pursuits and cleanse our sacred spaces for the part of the year when we spend most of our time indoors.

The nights lengthen and the veil between the worlds grows thin. It is traditionally a time when Pagans pay tribute to our ancestors. We explore new ways of honoring and connecting with those who have gone before. We also show our respect for our descendants, sharing our spirituality and religion with our children. Where our celebrations intersect with popular culture, such as the secular holiday of Halloween, we offer our knowledge to those who are interested in learning more about our traditions and practices.

Samhain is known as a 'time outside of time.' Some Pagans consider all the days between Samhain and Yule as part of the void, a break before the sun cycle begins anew. During this darkest time of the year we look deeply within ourselves. Rather than despairing, we look to the darkness as a time of respite, during which we rest, reflect and restore our spirits. We connect with self and deity in a quieter way, perhaps connecting with the Goddess as the Dark Mother. We use divination to help us choose a path or see into a possible future. Even as we enter the void, we keep our thoughts and actions positive, knowing that we are always moving toward our goals. We strive to stay hopeful even in difficult or trying situations.

Samhain 1997: House Cleansing

All life is sacred, as are all places. Yet it's beneficial to clean and purify the spaces we set aside for various purposes. Mother Earth does this quite naturally on a regular basis. From cleansing rain to gusty winds to the forest fires that scour our landscape, the earth seems to know when she needs to start fresh at a certain location.

At this time of year, when we spend more time indoors in our chosen places of shelter, we should remember the need to clean our sacred spaces, physically as well as spiritually. This is probably where the idea of fall and spring cleaning came from; our ancestors noted the need for seasonal cleansing of the places where they ate, slept, dreamed and worked.

When giving your home a good psychic cleanse, think about the purpose of each room. You might see your living room as a welcoming space where friends meet, or as a quiet retreat where you can relax on a winter night. The bedroom is often the inner sanctum of your space, set aside for sleep, dreams and making love. Some people are fortunate enough to have a room specifically intended for ritual and meditation. As you clean each room, hold your intent in your mind like a mantra. That will help give root to the energy that you plant there.

There are many methods to use when purifying your home. Each cleansing should be preceded by a mundane house-cleaning (tidy, do dishes, dust, vacuum, the whole works). Then cleanse yourself with a bath or shower and establish sacred space in your preferred manner. Now you can proceed through your home, focusing on each room in turn. Author Denise Linn, in her book *Sacred Space*, offers a variety of ideas for cleansing. Methods that I usually include during a cleansing ritual are smudging, drumming or chanting the energy of each room and sprinkling blessed salt water in the corners.

If you haven't done so before, a home cleansing is a perfect time to call on land and house guardians, spirits who, in exchange for offerings of food, drink and space, will guard your home and its inhabitants. If you do have relationships with your guardians, remember to honor them during the cleansing and thank them for their blessings. For more details about home guardians and how to work with them, you might want to read *The Pagan Family* by Ceisiwr Serith.

It's also beneficial to cast a circle that psychically encompasses your whole dwelling. If you occupy an entire house and some land, it's a good idea to walk the perimeters and perhaps place stones or other markers around them. You can also include physical reminders of your cleansing inside your home, anything from special crystals, to copper pennies over each door and window ledge, to burning your favorite incense each day.

We each also have sacred space within us, where we can be alone with our thoughts and meditations. At Samhain, we have the opportunity to draw inside ourselves a bit and welcome the more introspective energies of winter. It's a good idea to cleanse your inner space, after what was perhaps a busy, social summer and fall. Meditate, get more rest, read, paint, compose music or whatever signals to you that it is time to go within and give yourself a chance to regroup. You might enjoy the New Year's tradition of making resolutions or perhaps just updating your goals and seeing what progress you have made.

May you have a magickal Samhain and may your hearth be warm and welcoming.

Samhain 1998: Pagan Parenting

As the working parent of a small child, I find that my days fill up quickly. Sometimes I feel that when time is short, what suffers is the time my family and I devote to our spiritual practices. But then my son (whose magickal name is Dryst until he is old enough to choose his own) does something that makes me feel like we are right on track.

The idea for this column came from one such recent incident. My husband Quester, who is a full-time Dad, took Dryst to the park one day. As they were walking along, Quester handed him a bottle of water. Dryst, who is two years old, took a sip and then deliberately spilled some onto the ground, saying 'water for Goddess,' then took another sip and said 'water for me.' He was pouring a libation, on his own initiative! He has seen us do this in the past, especially on hikes in the woods, but not recently enough for it to be just copycat behavior. He thought of it and acted upon it. Hearing this was one of those times when all the joys of parenting open up before me and I'm happy to be able to share my spirituality with my son.

It's interesting to me how early he has shown an interest in things magickal. He loves to sit with me during my daily Tarot ritual (a three-card reading each morning) and carefully hold each of the cards in turn. When a good friend of ours comes to visit, Dryst draws daily runes with him, dropping whatever toy he's playing with to go sit on his lap. Dryst shares my fondness for picking up pretty rocks, shells and feathers that I encounter on walks. He'll bring one over to me with a big smile: 'Rock for you, Mommy!' And since he could speak his first few words, he's noticed the moon in the sky and pointed a tiny finger with an excited 'moon!' – whether it was a crescent, half or full moon.

I've always thought it was wrong of parents to force their religion upon their kids. I was not raised within a religious tradition, so when I was a kid and had friends or classmates who had to wear skirts every day, couldn't go dancing or had to go to church and religious classes every week, I thought they were being treated unfairly. That's why I'm going to teach my children the basics about the major world religions and their beliefs and practices, show them where to turn if they want more information, and make sure they know that religion is their own personal choice.

But that doesn't mean that I won't share my own spirituality with them, and in fact it would be hard not to do so. I think children are 'natural Pagans,' tuned in to nature and its wonders. When they are young, especially, children love 'sacred play' and family traditions and rituals. So I'm already sharing with Dryst aspects of my own religion. As long as I make sure that as he matures, he knows it is his own choice what to believe and practice, I think having his roots in an earth-based spirituality will bring him many gifts. Not the least of which are an open mind and an open heart.

Samhain 1999: Samhain and Popular Culture

As we celebrate Samhain, arguably the most important Sabbat of the Wheel, we are surrounded by our culture's secular celebration of what is known as Halloween. The question, especially for those of us who are parents, is what to do about the convergence of these two holidays (something we face again at Yuletide). How and what will we celebrate?

I know some Pagans who want nothing to do with the secular traditions of Halloween. They feel that the images and symbols, particularly of witches, have been perverted and that there is a lack of respect for our religion. They also feel, and rightly so, that the holiday has been consumerized by our culture to the point where the plastic-costume-makers, candy companies and dentists are the only ones who benefit from the focus on 'treats' for kids.

On the other end of the spectrum, I have friends who embrace the secular images of Halloween as part of their celebration, thus transforming them. Dressing up in costumes, even those of traditional scary witches, faeries or monsters, can bring a sense of mirth to our rituals. And these traditions, such as wearing masks and sharing delicious food on this final harvest of the year, do have roots in ancient traditions. One friend in particular, who has a great sense of childlike joy about this holiday, lets her trickster self go wild on this night and yet manages to instill a sense of respect for Samhain in her non-Pagan friends and family.

Personally, I'm somewhere in the middle. Quester and I do plan to take our kids, who are still small, trick-or-treating (with homemade costumes); we'll also include them in the Samhain festivities, to the extent they can understand. I don't usually dress up in a costume for the holiday, but I may do so this year, since we're having a party. If I do, I'll go with the neo-Pagan custom of dressing to reflect symbolically what I'd like to accomplish or become in the new year. We are having a Samhain party, which will include a ritual, to which Pagans and some non-Pagans are invited. We'll honor the ancestors and do some scrying, as well as sharing a potluck feast.

Samhain presents an opportunity for us, as Pagans, to educate others about our beliefs and practices. In recent years, many well-known witches have appeared in the mainstream media at Samhain and have presented an articulate vision of what we are really all about. I think that gradually the images of witches as 'ugly creatures of evil' are being replaced by a growing awareness about nature religions. Don't get me wrong; I know there is still a long way to go. But perhaps instead of being offended at the lack of respect our honored traditions are given, we can use this time of year as an opportunity to educate. I think in most cases the ignorance is genuine. Yes, there are those who are still hostile to us and believe we are working with their devil to perpetuate lies. But they are, happily, not in the majority.

The convergence of Samhain and Halloween doesn't have to be annoying or inconvenient. It can be a chance to include both mirth and reverence in our celebrations, to 'lighten up' this dark time of the year. For those who have children, you can include secular celebrations if you're comfortable with them, but also share your Pagan beliefs and rites. As our kids get older, we plan to explain to them the origins of the various customs and how some of them are indeed perversions of the rites of ancient days.

And through a gentle education of the general public, whether in the media or simply among your non-Pagan friends, this holiday can provide a golden opportunity to describe what we do and why.

Samhain 2000: The Dark Mother

Now is the time of the year when the Goddess, in her aspect of Dark Mother, makes her appearance. The harvest is done and we settle in for the long hard winter. All that was born in the spring and flourished through the summer, brought to fruition at the time of the harvest, must now begin to die. The physical darkness comes earlier each day. Rather than dread the approach of winter, we can welcome this aspect of the Goddess and let her help us with our spiritual work.

Something the Dark Mother, or Crone, is especially good at is winnowing. What is it that we need to winnow or purge in our lives at this time? What part of your life can you destroy? Sometimes we have addictions we need to purposefully get rid of. Maybe addictions is too strong a word; perhaps they are just behaviors that have somehow become habits. Examine your daily actions, your mental constructs, even your spiritual disciplines. Is there something that may have once been good for you that you have now simply grown beyond?

Call on the Dark Mother, she who fiercely guards the tender, fragile parts of yourself, to destroy that which is harmful on any level. Invoking her at the waning moon, in this waning time of year, is even more powerful. Find that one thing that you wish to be rid of and perform a banishing ritual. You might want to find a symbol of the habit or behavior that you have outgrown and then burn or bury it as part of your ritual. Or you can write it down on a piece of paper and consign that to the flames.

Call on the Crone at this time of the year as the Hermit, one who turns inward. The cold fall evenings are an ideal time for introspection. Examine those fragile or hidden parts of your nature. What can you do to nurture the secret aspects of yourself? How still and quiet can you be? Invite yourself to take more time than usual for rest and meditation. Explore your personal mysteries. The dark night sky can help us see the tiny flame at the core of the soul.

The Dark Mother can also help us to reach out to those who have crossed over to the other side. The Crone can pass with ease through the veil between the worlds, which is especially thin at Samhain, and enable us to communicate with the spirits of loved ones. Invoke her before scrying or ask for her aid as you do magick to recognize and honor your ancestors. Watch for her presence in your dreams and see who accompanies her. Make room for messages sent to you through her presence.

Open your heart to the Dark Mother this Samhain season and see what richness arises in your spirit. Rather than fearing the dark parts of yourself or of the earth, consciously honor the dark time of year as an integral part of the Wheel. Death on any level also brings transformation, from which the light is born once again. Enjoy your journey, with the Goddess, into the depths of your being. See you on the other side.

Samhain 2002: Touching the Gods

As we enter the dark time of the year, I find myself becoming more contemplative. Recently, when pondering what the divine is to me, I realized that it is actually a feeling. What I believe is that everything we see and experience, and many other things we don't know, are all a sacred expression of the divine essence. But to know it intellectually is one thing, and those moments of feeling it, of knowing it to be true in my heart, body, mind and spirit, are something else altogether.

The divine feels like the warm comforting breath of the Goddess. I glimpse it in moments of synchronicity, when the crow feather on the trail catches my eye. I visit the feeling in dreams, riding the waves of sky. I travel there in meditation, when my breath connects with Her rhythm. I'm swept away on tides of bliss when I dance with the God to flowing grooves. The feeling crashes over me in the ecstasy of orgasm, wrapped in a lover's arms and legs and aura. Sometimes as I do my yoga or walk in the sunshine, the feeling holds me up, a light drifting motion.

I know this energy is always present; we are all composed of divine matter, both light and shadow. Not only the birds and trees and the ocean, but also cars and neon signs and crumpled McDonald's bags in the street: all of it is part of the divine. What is hard at times is remembering, recognizing how the pattern fits together and how we are in harmony with the whole. It's not something that can be forced and, in fact, when I try too hard to make the connection, the striving can push me further away. All I can do is provide the setting that works for me, with symbols that remind me of the feeling. I can use the techniques that bring me to a receptive, relaxed yet aware state of mind: breathing deeply, listening to peaceful music, gazing at the trees, the clouds or a candle flame.

When I feel the divine all around me, pervading me, what does it feel like? Like gazing into the eyes of a new lover, like being caressed gently, like unconditional love. I feel lighter and a gentle smile feels natural on my face. There is a buoyant joy and my thoughts seem to relax too, leaving more space in my mind for just being. There is a lack of urgency and a dropping away of self-consciousness. I am quick to laugh, make eye contact and share my joy with other beings.

Sometimes I wonder why I can't sustain the feeling and go through life aware, in a conscious way, that everything is sacred. But I think we come to this physical life to learn lessons. Perhaps this is the key lesson we are learning to embody. We plunge ourselves into space and time, into a body, distancing ourselves, at least as we perceive it, from our source. Then it's our task to remember that we *are* the source, that the divine is everywhere we travel.

As human beings, we are all at different stages on the continuum of learning to remember. I find that I also experience things in cycles; there are times when the connection is made effortlessly and often; and other parts of the cycle when, even with frequent prayer and meditation, the feeling remains elusive. Cultivating a detached, compassionate awareness is all I can do at those times. When I grasp at those joyous moments of experiencing the divine, they fade rapidly away.

What I've learned recently is that the practice of mindfulness, of being in the moment and accepting whatever arises, allows the Goddess-moments a landing pad, a lovely petal on which they can alight like a timid butterfly. And that just the briefest moments of that divine feeling can sustain me through many moons of the long winter of my soul.

Samhain 2003: Pagan Homeschooling

As Mom to two young homeschooled kids, I'm noticing lately how much homeschooling and Pagan spirituality have in common. Once seen as the domain of Christians who kept their kids home to indoctrinate them into Creationism, homeschooling, much like Paganism, has begun to garner more mainstream awareness in recent years. Homeschoolers choose their path for many reasons, as do Pagans. Some values that both hold in common include an emphasis on self-determination, an eagerness to explore the world for oneself rather than being told what to believe and the desire to tailor one's studies to the individual rather than a group. Freedom is a key tenet.

Home education encompasses a wide variety of methods. Some homeschooling families adopt a structured approach, using a set curriculum, much like seekers who study with a traditional three-degree circle. Others are more independent, crafting their studies in a child-led, eclectic approach which reminds me of my own independent studies as a solitary Pagan. Both homeschoolers and Pagans use books, the Internet and contacts with people in the community to gather ideas and find support.

Like Paganism, homeschooling requires a leap of faith and the belief that you'll be guided to the best approach for you and your kids. This, of course, includes maintaining that faith during times of doubt, when things don't seem to be going as well as you'd hoped. Misunderstandings about homeschooling, similar to those attached to Paganism, often lead some family members to be, shall we say, less than supportive. Both Pagans and homeschoolers tend to surround themselves with an intentional community full of people who understand and support their choices.

The essence of homeschooling, like magick, is in the practice and mastery of certain basic concepts. Once a child has learned to read, write and do basic math, the sky's the limit. Learning how to do research and then following your interests and inclinations will not only lead to a well-rounded education, but will also bring joy and connection as you explore the world. Like most Pagans I know, homeschoolers love to celebrate holidays and the changes of season and to learn about the traditions of other cultures.

In my experience, Pagan spirituality and homeschooling are a terrific combination. As this Samhain season approaches, my family is busy making costumes (a medieval princess and 'an archer like Robin Hood'), carving pumpkins, learning how to make piecrust so we can bake homemade pumpkin pies, planning games and crafts for a children's Samhain party, reading Halloween story books from the library and designing a cool scarecrow. I'm glad that both our religion and our approach to learning allow plenty of time and energy for an independent, creative exploration of life.

Samhain 2004: A Turning Point

The dark time of the year, between Samhain and Yule, is upon us, and I can certainly feel the change in the air. Not just the weather, with chilly days and longer nights, but also in my own activities and desires. On the one hand there is 'bringing in the last harvest,' which in our modern world translates to preparing the house and garden for winter, getting in the last hikes and other outdoor activities while the weather permits, and perhaps canning or freezing vegetables. Then, of course, on the other hand there are the traditional preparations for the winter holidays and the celebrations with family and friends. But in balance to that hectic activity is the desire to turn inward, to begin a hibernation of sorts.

The ability to accept and be comfortable with paradox has been cited as a sign of enlightenment. Samhain is a Sabbat that can certainly help us with that notion. It is the final harvest, when the days are getting shorter and the dark half of the year begins. It is a time for letting go, for releasing that which we don't need and letting it die away, much as the trees release their leaves. But Samhain is also known as the Celtic New Year, when we can sow our hopes and wishes for the next turn of the Wheel, like the winter crops that were sown at this time of year to lie dormant for the winter months and begin to spring up near Imbolc (in the British Isles, though not until later in harsher climates).

Samhain is a turning point, a time of transformation, a gateway. It is one of the times when the veil between the worlds is thin. We honor our ancestors and can contact them if they wish, perhaps to ask for their advice. We can use divination to help us choose a path or see into a possible future. Samhain Eve is known as a 'time outside of time,' and some beliefs extend that to all the days between Samhain and Yule.

This time of year is a good one for meditation and intro-spection. Take the time to sit quietly and allow your conscious thoughts to drop away. Find a comfortable position and focus on your breathing. You may hear wise words from the Goddess in her Crone aspect or from an ancestor or spirit guide. You might catch a glimpse of future events. Or at the very least, you'll become centered and relaxed and you'll be honoring your body's natural desire for rest and quiet at this time of year.

Many of us have busy lives, with obligations and projects that fill up our days. Yet it is important to balance this activity with rest. The darkest part of the year reminds us that it is necessary to take time to ourselves, to recharge our batteries. Perhaps you don't wish for a complete hibernation, but as the days grow short, you can plan at least some uninterrupted time at home.

As you relax into your mini-hibernation, take the time to embrace the paradox at the heart of this turn of the Wheel of the Year. Release something that you no longer need, allowing it to die away and be gone from your life. This will create a space which you can then fill with a wish or hope for the new turn of the Wheel. Let go of the old while inviting in the new. Some people like to make a vow of some sort, like a resolution for the New Year. It could relate to letting go, such as abstaining from alcohol or sugar from Samhain until Yule. Or it could be a part of a new goal, like taking a class or volunteering your time for a worthy cause.

After a very busy and stressful year, I plan to devote more time to my yoga practice and to explore some new avenues for creativity. I also hope to release some fears and worries that are lingering in my psyche. What will you release and draw to you in the coming months? If you don't know, then all the better, for now is the perfect time to rest in the moment between seasons, allowing yourself to be open to the energies of beings from beyond the veil and to divine your soul's calling. I wish you the best this season.

Samhain 2005: In Defense of Optimism

The place to improve the world is first in one's own heart and head and hands, and then work outward from there.
Robert M. Pirsig

From time to time, I hear (or read) Pagans talking about 'fluffy bunny witches,' those whom they feel are shallow in their practice of magick, usually because of an optimistic viewpoint on a serious or troubling topic. If Pagans make comments about how 'it's all about love, really' or 'we should forgive our enemies' or the like, some people assume that they aren't willing or able to deal with the darker aspects of the universe.

As an optimist who has endured some serious challenges and troubles over the past couple of years and has emerged stronger and still filled with hope, I'd like to offer my take on this phenomenon. I'm not saying that everyone who calls herself a Pagan is fully committed to the hard work of self-growth. There will always be 'wanna-be' Pagans who think it's cool to be a witch and beginners who are just stepping onto the path. But there are those of us who consistently focus on the positive, while still actively doing the spiritual work that we are called to do.

It's a basic tenet of magick that a clear focus on the intent is what will help our spells succeed. Even in mainstream culture, 'the power of positive thinking' is known to enhance health and reduce emotional stress. In a frightening or upsetting situation, whether personal or global, it's even more important to maintain a focus on your goals and values.

The 'War on Terrorism' is one example. No matter your political persuasion, it's easy to be drawn into worry and fear about when and where 'they' will strike next. Yet if we allow ourselves to dwell in that fear, the energy we have for other projects is dissipated. Isn't it more productive in the long run to work for the change that we feel will make the world ultimately safer? It could be helping to eliminate world hunger and disease, providing support to the US military troops or whatever seems right to you. A positive outlook, grounded in actions taken to create the change you feel is needed, is far more effective than constant worrying.

As the saying goes, 'be the change you wish to create.' Many

Pagans are activists working for peace and justice. Yet lots of them are chronically stressed and angry, burnt out from not practicing self-care as they pursue this calling. Granted, there are many things going on in the world that are destructive and cruel. But if you feed into that negative energy, you're adding to it, rather than creating a true change.

I fully believe that focusing on the positive does more for the greater whole. The energy that we put out into the web of life will resonate in the lives of others, affecting them in surprising and positive ways, and as that effect spreads, we begin to see it in our culture's worldview. As astrologer and author Rob Brezsny notes, 'Today the conventional wisdom is that everything is falling apart, that the world is a terrible place to live, that bad things predominate. The most taboo possibility of all is the idea that the world is full of beauty and that life is on our side.'

This doesn't mean putting on a false front of 'everything will be just fine.' It does, at times, take a focused effort to find your center and look to the hopeful side of a difficult situation. But as long as you keep listening to your soul, your intuition, your calling and follow through with the necessary work, the Goddess won't steer you wrong. And when you hear other Pagans express hope and love under difficult circumstances, rather than assume their outlook is shallow, take a moment to appreciate the 'fluffy bunny effect.' It might just brighten your day when you need it most.

Samhain 2006: Touching the Ancestors

As the Wheel of the Year winds down and the earth prepares to sleep, it's time to turn our thoughts to Samhain. Traditionally, this is a holiday when Pagans honor our ancestors and beloved dead, while the veil between the worlds is thin and the dark nights grow longer. Often this means cooking their favorite foods and setting a place for them at the Samhain feast. But what are some other ways to honor and connect with those who have crossed over?

If you have friends or family members who have passed away within the past few years, perhaps you wish to create something new to honor their memory. Writing a poem or song, embroidering a wall hanging or building a rock garden are some examples of creative tributes. Use your imagination and, as you work, focus on happy memories of times you spent with your loved one. If you like, charge your creation in sacred space, dedicating it to the spirit of the person it's made for.

Another way to honor your ancestors is to find out new things about them. Ask your elders about people in your family or community you were too young to know or remember. You may discover many funny or poignant stories by asking questions and then sitting back and just listening. At a recent family gathering, I discovered that the cat symbol I have drawn since I was a kid (and which contributed to my choice of Pagan name) came from times I spent drawing with my Mom's favorite eccentric aunt when I was really little. I'll certainly be honoring Great Aunt Ruby as part of my Samhain ritual this year!

You can also, with a little research, discover something new about your family's culture of origin. Go beyond the stereotypes of what it means to be of French or Celtic or African descent, perhaps unearthing an old song or folk tradition that you can use in your Samhain celebration. Or dig a bit deeper and discover the reason why a particular custom or tradition was handed down as part of the culture's lore.

Many of us also honor spiritual ancestors, who may or may not be blood-related. Who are those who went before, whose lives have brought meaning to your own? Women during the Burning Times? The anonymous conductors for the Underground Railroad? Native Americans who walked this land centuries ago? Find a way to honor them this Samhain, perhaps leaving an offering in the woods or garden. Find or create a piece of jewelry to wear as a tribute to them or burn a candle on your altar in their memory on the days leading up to Samhain.

There are many ways to honor our beloved dead. Samhain is an especially good time to do so, but it's also important to remember them throughout the Wheel of the Year. Perhaps you could set up an altar or shrine of photographs and special items passed down from past generations. Or simply send them a prayer, song or mental 'thank you' when you think of them. By remembering our ancestors and paying tribute to them in some way, we continue the thread of love and magick woven through the tapestry of our lives, passing it along eventually to those who come after us and continuing the legacy of our evolving spirituality.

Samhain 2007: Positive Magick

This is the darkest time of year. The days are short and the nights are getting cold. We are bracing ourselves, physically and mentally, for the cold winter to come. Darkness, however, doesn't have to mean pain or negativity. We create our circumstances through our attitudes and the energy we put out into the world. Be positive and instead look to darkness as a respite, the night during which we rest, reflect and restore our spirits.

Magick isn't just what we do during a ritual or when we are in a cast circle. We live our magick all the time, expressing our unique creative energies wherever we go and whatever we do. Even those of us who are longtime practicing Pagans can get into a pattern where we are focused on lack, problems and negativity in our lives and the world. We complain or lament and express, through words and actions, our ego's fears and worries. Yet by doing so, we are attracting more of those energies to us. Don't we know better than that?

I'm not saying it's easy or that we should put on a mask of happiness and contentment. If we experience emotions such as anger, disappointment or fear, we can express them in a way that allows them to move through us and then out again. If we cling or become attached too strongly to our notions of lack and negativity, we will manifest more of those situations in our daily lives. If we bury those emotions without dealing with them at all, we are holding onto them in our bodies and they can manifest as illness and dis-ease. It's the Threefold Law in action. That which you put out into the world, or into your inner world, returns to you threefold.

It's easy to get caught in a pattern of negativity without realizing it. Take a day where you focus on listening to yourself. Without trying to change them, just listen to the words you say to others throughout your day and to the thoughts in your head. Observe the things you are creating with your words, particularly if they are negative in tone: 'I'm having such a bad day today.' 'I don't have enough money.' 'He's late again; he's always so inconsiderate.' 'I hate this weather.' 'I don't feel well.' 'This isn't what I wanted.'

The next step is to begin to turn those thoughts and words around. When you notice this behavior, stop yourself gently, without being angry or disappointed that you were being negative. Think of a creative way to phrase what you're saying or thinking, one that will begin to change or improve your situation: 'I'm learning a lot from these challenges.' 'I have what I need.' 'I'm supported by the abundance of the universe.' 'He wants to spend time with me and will be here when he can.' 'The rain is feeding the trees and plants.' 'I'm taking care of my body and encouraging healing.' 'I'm focused on manifesting my desires.' It will feel a bit awkward at first, but practice 'acting as if.' Imagine that your words and thoughts are immediately going to work to create a better day. The more you practice, the more it will become a mental habit.

When you have thoughts or emotions that you consider negative, don't leap to judge or censor them. Don't become attached to them or identify yourself as a victim, either. Simply let them be. Mentally say to yourself 'thank you for that information' or 'thanks for sharing.' Allow yourself to continue to learn how to be fully you, how to best express your energies in the world.

At this dark time of the year, rather than worrying about the cold or wishing for the warmer and sunnier days, take time to rest. Sleep longer. Stay at home and do things that are comforting to you: take a hot bath, read a good book, watch a favorite movie, eat hot soup and fresh bread, have your favorite dessert, do yoga. If you feel sad, have a good cry and then let it go. Write or draw your difficult or uncomfortable feelings and then burn the paper to release those energies back into the cosmos. Invent private rituals to connect with the divine and with your soul's deepest wishes. Think of new ways to rejuvenate and restore your spirit. By being creative and nurturing yourself, you will experience joy and wonder and learning, and soon your daily life will reflect and embody that which you most wish to create.

Samhain 2008: A Mindful Retreat

Samhain is a natural time for introspection. As the earth turns inward once again, so we too have the urge to go within, to explore the inner reaches of our self and to rest from being active in the world. We retreat from our activity in the outer realms or we feel the impulse to do so.

What does the word 'retreat' mean to you? In the wider culture, it can have a negative connotation. We may 'retreat into our own little world' when stung by events involving relationships. Armies make their retreat when they are losing the battle. Yet a thoughtful retreat from our daily activities is necessary to keep our spirits cleansed and centered.

When you think 'retreat,' you may get images of an airy building, filled with calm people twisting their bodies into yoga postures or meditating silently on a wooden floor in a beam of sunlight. That's where I'm headed, just days after I write these words, for that's what calls to me. But a retreat can be as simple as taking an afternoon to turn off the phone and TV, relax in a hot bath and write in your journal.

Our impulse for retreat, rest and introspection can be difficult to honor in this culture. We work long days, then fill our evenings and weekends with social events, volunteering and errands. What happens to our need for quiet, especially in this season? It is something important to prioritize, to ensure that it happens before we become stressed out or ill. We've all heard the advice 'schedule time for yourself in your appointment book,' and perhaps even laughed or rolled our eyes. But why not? Isn't our own well-being and centeredness a key part of what we bring to the world?

I find that when I have alone time, I often spend it reading fiction. Others like to watch movies or TV, or play video games. While relaxing is enjoyable, it isn't the same as taking time to be introspective. We're still focused on *others'* creations and perceptions of the world. Next time you have that opportunity, choose something that focuses on *you*, on your own thoughts, feelings, ideas and energies. Meditate, take a walk, paint or draw or make music. Something that, while being restful, also allows your unique spirit to play and stretch. You are the most important being in your life, for without you, how could you perceive anything else in the universe?

Samhain is the perfect time to renew your focus on introspection. Make a commitment to yourself and take time out on a regular basis. Sign up for that weekend at a retreat center, if it appeals to you, or rent or borrow a cabin in the woods where you can feed the woodstove, eat simple foods and walk by a lake. If you are an extrovert by nature, retreating in the company of others, perhaps by taking a meditation class, can be inspiring. It provides a place where you know you can sit in fellowship, yet undisturbed, for an hour or so each week.

The hard part is often just getting yourself motivated. Once you feel the rewards of taking time to go within, you'll want to keep it up. As you enjoy Samhain, remember to reflect not only on your ancestors, but also upon yourself and your own path.

Chapter 2

Yule

Yule is the celebration of the Winter Solstice, the longest night of the year. It heralds the official arrival of winter and also the return of the light, when the days begin to grow longer again and signal the eventual return of spring. Yule is part of the festival of light, the winter holiday season which includes celebrations from many cultures, such as Christmas (which in my extended clan is a secular family-oriented holiday), Chanukah, Boxing Day, Kwanzaa and New Year's Day. Also taking place at Yuletide is the Roman celebration of Saturnalia, when normal social roles were reversed and all members of society were encouraged to eat, drink and be merry.

Most ancient celebrations at this time of year were about coming together as a community, to hope for and then celebrate the return of the sun's light. Winter holiday traditions, such as serving special meals and giving gifts to family and friends, are ways of showing our caring and gratitude for our loved ones.

In my community, our Yule ritual includes lighting a bonfire. We then hold a vigil throughout the longest night, lending our support to the Goddess as She labors to give birth to the Sun God. We keep the fire burning, with some folks staying up all night to greet the dawn and others welcoming the sun in their dreams. When the rising sun shows that the God has been reborn, we close the circle and celebrate with breakfast and a long nap.

Yet there is a contrast at this time of year between our celebrations in community and our desire to hibernate. In my own practice, I've had to continually refocus on finding balance between the secular holiday season's busy preparations and my own need for a quieter focus. We are all ultimately solitary practitioners, finding our own path of connection with the divine, and we must each balance serving the community with our own solo pursuits. Some ways to nurture ourselves at this time of year include introspection, dream work and keeping a Book of Shadows. We might choose to purify ourselves in the time between Samhain and Yule, testing our will and centering ourselves in healthy practices. Self-care is particularly important if we are in the midst of adjusting to changes in our lives.

Yule can also be a time of magick and enchantment. Seen through a child's eyes, the myths and stories of this time of year are full of awe and wonder. Many of our traditions focus on that surge of joy and hope, and on a new way of seeing things. We can find that sort of magick in our everyday lives, not only at Yule but throughout the Wheel of the Year.

Yule 1997: A Quieter Holiday Season

It is the dark time of the year, just now beginning to give us hope with the turn toward the light and the renewal and rebirth of the God, yet also the beginning of the hardest part of winter. It is ostensibly the time when we withdraw and turn inward. Why, then, do most of us find ourselves so busy at this time of the year?

Part of it is certainly our involvement in the customs of the secular American culture. Most of us have extended families who expect us to attend Thanksgiving, Christmas and New Year's celebrations. Many of us are invited to parties by friends and employers, and go out shopping for holiday gifts for our loved ones. And that's not even taking into account our own planning for Winter Solstice rituals and gatherings. It is one of the busiest and, yes, most stressful times of year for many people.

I believe that there have always been 'festivals of light,' Pagan celebrations at the time of year when the days began to get longer. But I think the contrast of those celebrations with the time of quiet rest and retreat that came before, and would come afterward, was part of what made them so special. In other words, if we go through the time from Samhain to Solstice and beyond with a calendar full of social engagements, traveling, decorating, shopping, cooking, making crafts and more, will we really be happy to celebrate the holidays when they finally arrive? Or will we be glad when they are over and done, so we can have a much-needed rest?

I'm not recommending giving up entirely the customs and traditions of the 'holiday season,' as it is now called (which I think is great: it puts Solstice and Chanukah on an equal footing with Christmas). Some of my favorite activities at this time of year include making gifts for people I love, going on walks in the city to look at all the lights and decorations, caroling and going to parties. I just think that we would do well to balance our activities with some time to ourselves.

How can we sustain and recapture the magickal aspects of the Winter Solstice and the dark part of the year? And, in doing so, how can we replenish our own energies?

Why do we hurtle ourselves through every inch of time and space? I must say around some corner I can sense a resting place.
Emily Saliers (The Indigo Girls, 'Get Out the Map,' from *Shaming of the Sun*).

It might be too late in this busy season to take time out to do the things that you love and that make you feel recharged (I'm making a note now to remind myself of this next Samhain). But that 'resting place' is coming: the rest of the long New England winter stretches ahead of us. Take the days after your celebration of Yule to wind down, to be with your inner circle of family and friends, those who understand if you want to sit and just be still. Do some private rituals. Sleep in whenever you can. Capture the joyful parts of the holidays and let them seep into your soul.

Personally, I plan to let the bear in me take over once the

preparations and celebrations are through. I have a happy vision of snuggling on the couch with a book and some leftover cookies, reading and daydreaming. In the meantime, I'm living in the moment, enjoying the fast pace, the cooking and card-making and gift-buying and the partying and dancing.

I hope all of you have a very magickal and joyful Yule! Blessed Be!

Yule 1998: Saturnalia Dream

I was uncertain what to write for this special Saturnalia issue of EarthTides, but then I was gifted with the following dream:

I am told by a friend that he has a connection with 'the Masons' and can get Quester and I an audience at their upcoming banquet. On the appointed evening he escorts us to a huge hall, filled with tables and chattering people. We are told to sit in chairs behind the diners at a table in the back of the hall, up on a dais. After a while they deign to speak with us. They ask questions of me. They want to know why I am here. I carefully open a small wooden box that I am holding in my lap; it is filled with treasures and artifacts that I recently found at the bottom of a warm sea. I select a small rose quartz replica of a castle and give it to them. It is placed in a basket of gems and jewels on the table. They are all delighted with my gift! We are told to pull up our chairs and join the feast.

The people at the banquet are mostly middle-aged and dressed as conventional business-men and -women, but they are merry and have a shimmering energy around them. I look out over the hall. It is decorated with strings of golden balls and pearls, blazing candles, jewels and hanging crystals. The whole place glitters golden, dazzling my senses.

Conversing pleasantly, my table-mates and I make our way to the buffet table, which is spread with a great feast. I fill my plate high with sweets and delicacies, and then realize that I am unbearably thirsty. I see punchbowls but no glasses, so I ask someone for a cup. I am told that we must provide our own cups. But being new, we did not bring cups. I put down my plate and go in search of the kitchen. It is a big empty echoing place. By looking carefully I finally find a thick clear dusty beer glass, like you'd see in a bar. I wash it off and make my way back to the table. But when I arrive, my magnificent meal has shrunk to a small piece of bread in the center of my plate.

Next I am relaxing on the grass in the courtyard, where some of the guests are picnicking. I sense that an initiation has begun. All is not as it seems. Quester is nowhere to be seen. I decide to climb a nearby tree, to get a vantage point from which to view the celebration. I climb up, but then the limb I'm perched on breaks and I tumble to the ground. I am unhurt and decide to keep the broken branch. But a nearby partygoer tells me that the tree belongs to a man who will soon return, and who will be angry that I have broken it. It contains magickal wax for use in his spells. To prove her point, she urges me to look into the branch, which I now notice is hollow. I look and am immediately blinded by a brilliant flash of light. The people around me all laugh. Just then the man returns, but he is not at all upset that I've broken his tree. He congratulates me and urges me to follow him. In a daze I move behind him towards the great hall. The dream fades and I awaken, knowing that I am somehow changed.

Yule 1999: Turning Inward: How to Get Through the Dark Time of Year

The focus this time of year is often on family, friends and service to the community. That's as it should be, but we sometimes go overboard, forgetting that this dark time of year is also intended for introspection and a healthy dose of self-nurturing. When you add to that the fact that it gets dark very early each day, and the temperatures are dropping, many of us start to feel a little down. And yet we expect ourselves to be superhuman in our efforts to make the holiday 'special.'

Last year I overextended myself. I had just moved to a new home and wanted to put on a fabulous holiday celebration for family and friends. I decorated and cooked and shopped and generally ran myself ragged. Sure enough, on the day after the party, I caught a virus and got violently ill (as did everyone in my household). When it has had enough, your body will force you to stop, sometimes in not-so-pleasant ways.

This year I've slowed down and have been taking time to smell the fir trees, as it were. And the holiday season has been much more enjoyable. Here are some tips to help you turn inward and get through the dark time of the year without being a Yuletide Scrooge:

- **Light candles.** Yeah, I know, we're Pagans, so we already do this. Well, light more candles.
- **Bundle up** for an evening walk in your town and enjoy the holiday lights and decorations. As you walk, meditate on the return of the light.
- **Read.** If you want to make this a family activity, read holiday books to the kids or to each other. Or just take time off from holiday preparations and curl up with a novel.
- **Make homemade gifts.** This is fun because you're doing things for others, yet you can spend time alone on quiet creative pursuits. As you work, you can focus on the person you're making the gift for or simply let your creative energies flow. Don't think of it (like I did last year) as just another task that needs to be done, but truly enjoy yourself.
- **Walk in the woods** and gather fir branches to decorate with. Be sure to gather fallen branches whenever possible, or ask permission of the tree and leave an offering. Smell the winter, taste the wind.
- **Write letters** to your loved ones describing how you feel about them. They will cherish this more than any gift you

could purchase.

- **Smile** at everyone you encounter, especially people who look stressed out. Share your light, joy and inner peace.
- **Make candles.** Give some away and save some to bless at Imbolc for use throughout the coming year.
- **Play holiday music** in your home. Turn off the TV or computer for the evening. Play games with your loved ones or put together a puzzle.
- **Celebrate.** Check into the (often free) holiday activities offered in your local area. They can be fun to attend and require no effort but getting there!
- **Create and perform a spell** to bring peace and balance to the world.
- **Feed the birds** and squirrels, or give them extra treats if you already do this. Weather permitting, leave milk and goodies out as offerings for the faeries.
- **Hold a Winter Solstice vigil** as part of your celebrations. Stay up until the sunrise or as late as you can before you curl up to sleep. Meditate on the turning of the Wheel.
- **Don't try to do all of these things.**

I hope these ideas help and that you have a lovely Yule. Blessings to you and yours!

Yule 2000: Gifts for Yourself

Last Yule, I wrote about how to slow down and enjoy the pleasures of the often-frenzied winter holiday season. The Wheel has turned once again and this year I find that I am, to a greater degree, taking my own advice. This year I've significantly reduced my holiday stress by reducing my expectations of what I should do.

This new way of approaching the winter holidays is connected to my vow at Samhain: increase my self-acceptance. For this Virgo, as one who is always striving for personal growth and improvement, it's a powerful goal. I read on a poster at a yoga class 'try to accept yourself, just as you are now, for 30 days.' I expanded this and made it my vow for the New Year. Most of the Pagans I know also try to continually progress along their spiritual paths, and while this is necessary and good, we should also acknowledge our good qualities, including the very fact that we are trying to improve.

When I first had the idea for this column, it sounded like an article in the December issue of a mainstream women's magazine: 'How to Pamper Yourself During the Holidays! Get a makeover! Buy a slinky new dress!' But this article will, I hope, be a little less materialistic. I hope it will help you in your own quest for self-acceptance. Below are some loving gifts you can give to yourself at this dark, cold time of year. Hopefully they will help encourage the return of the light, within and without, as the Wheel turns.

- **Dreamwork.** At this time of year, when the days are at their shortest, consider working with your dreams. Keep a dream journal and focus on intentions before you go to sleep at night. If you already do so, go deeper into your dreamwork practice. Try to work with lucid dreaming and with dream spellwork. There are several good books on this subject, including *Sacred Sleep: Dreams & the Divine* by Scott Cunningham.
- **Extra sleep.** While you're at it, get an extra hour of sleep each night. Many people can't alter their routine by sleeping in, but why not go to bed an hour early each night? Even if you're a night owl, like I am, get into bed early and read a book.
- **Meditation.** Add meditation to your routine or try new forms of meditation. It's a good time of year to do candle meditation, focusing on the return of the light. Hold the warmth of the flame within you.

- **Soup.** On one of these cold dark nights, make a pot of your favorite soup or other hot comforting meal. Savor it slowly, bite by bite, and feel it nourishing your body and soul. If you are more into sweets, make a batch of cookies and eat several, without guilt.
- **Silence.** Add some silence to your day. Shut off the radio in the car, or go without TV or music when you are at home. Go for a walk and listen to the myriad sounds of the natural world. Take a break from 'daily news,' especially political news. Talk less and ponder more.
- **Play time.** What do you love to do? What would you play if you were a child and had a couple of free hours? Frolic in the snow, get out some finger-paints or just toss a ball around. Whatever you choose. Enlist a friend if you want. Play freely for as long as you like.
- **A day off.** If at all possible, take an entire day off from work, school or your daily activities to do nothing or anything. Don't do holiday shopping or the laundry unless that is truly what calls to you. What a luxury this is. Enjoy it. If, like me, this is difficult to do because you have young children, involve them in your day off. Compromise with them on the fun activities you'll do on this special day.

Blessings to you and yours at Yule and always.

Yule 2001: Blessings of Community

Often at this time of year I counsel slowing down, becoming more introspective and heeding the pull of the dark part of the Wheel of the Year. This advice, which I strive to follow, comes in part as a reaction to the mainstream culture's emphasis on a frenzy of activity during the winter holidays.

And yet the most ancient celebrations at this time were about coming together as a community, to hope for and then celebrate the return of the sun's light. Recently I've been reflecting on the importance of community in my life. Unlike people in past centuries, much of what I consider my spiritual community does not consist of those people who live next door or nearby. Yet the bonds are strong on many levels. Even the introverts among us seek out others for fellowship and mutual support.

When we do ritual in a group over time, the community forms its own consciousness or 'group mind.' That mind is working even when we are not consciously aware of it. This can result in amusing synchronicities, like recently when I e-mailed a coven member who is often online with a brief note to 'call me.' When the phone rang less than five minutes later, I assumed he was replying to my note. But during our conversation, he started to laugh, saying that the e-mail I sent had just popped into his inbox.

These connections to our close friends are what enables us to 'lose ourselves' during energy work in circle. We become one…or, more accurately, we recognize our underlying unity, rather than focusing on the differences between us. It is a gift to be part of a close-knit group like this. And when, as is the case with any group of human beings, conflicts and problems come up, it is these very bonds that keep us moving forward and working to resolve them, even when we are emotionally weary or frustrated.

But how do we balance the demands and pleasures of being part of a community with the need for essential 'down time,' particularly at this time of year?

I find it is important to be clear about your needs and bound-aries. Rather than over-commit, or simply decline an invitation, explain that you need some time to recharge yourself. As any time-management guru would tell you, it helps to schedule time with yourself as a regular part of your week. Really. It helps no one if you are giving and doing so much that all your energy is dissipated. And when your friends know that Tuesday night is your night to be alone, they'll remember and respect that sacred space.

If you like to participate in holiday rituals such as gift-giving, making homemade gifts is an excellent way to be connected. Quester and I make personalized collage cards for family and friends each year, and the time we spend relaxed and focused on each individual, while snug and cozy in our living room, is both social and private. I also bake goodies to give away, and the care and attention I bring to this solo task not only spreads outward to the recipient, but gives me quiet time to reflect and meditate on the task at hand.

I also find that I move in cycles, often with the moon's phases, in terms of focusing outward on the community or being more inward-looking. Some weekends are a merry-go-round of activity and others become a retreat to the island of home, with time to read, get extra sleep and center myself.

Being part of a strong magickal community is both rewarding and complex. Particularly at this time of year, one must strike a balance between participation in the clan and the need to rest in the womb of the Goddess. Without withdrawing our attention from our loved ones, it is possible to rest and recharge, emerging re-inspired and with even more to contribute.

Happy Yule to you and yours!

Yule 2002: A Solstice Tale

Her belly is very large now and the skin is tight. The Lady steps carefully on Her walks through the icy forest each short, bright day. Some evenings, She putters restlessly about the cottage, tidying and cleaning. Other evenings She can do nothing more than drowse by the fire, Her book lying forgotten at her side. In meditation, She can sense the light within Her, the life almost ready to come forth. He seems, like Her, to be restless on some days, pushing and kicking from within and to be resting on others, gathering His energy as He prepares to be born. She smiles as She pictures holding Him close in Her arms.

It is dark and quiet inside Her womb. The baby Sun God sighs and wiggles a bit, trying to find a more comfortable position. He knows something is about to happen. He can feel the pressure building, and while He doesn't know quite what to expect, He is filled with excitement. He likes it when there is movement outside and that lovely humming noise She makes when She is busy. It lulls Him to sleep and brings Him dreams of brightness and wonder. When all is still, He listens to Her heartbeat and waits.

The people are preparing for Yule. They rush around, finding the perfect gift for a loved one, decorating their homes, baking the special treats of the season. Often they are busy, yet at other times they sit before the lighted tree, breathing slowly and listening to carols. They may curl up with a good book during the long, dark evenings. And those who listen carefully know that something is about to happen. The world is still and dark, even in the light of the swelling moon. Everything is poised, ready for what will happen next.

The people gather together to celebrate the Winter Solstice. They light candles in the darkness and some hold vigil throughout the longest night. The Lady is consumed with Her labor. She goes deep within, to a place of inner strength. She paces and breathes, panting and moaning. The baby God is ready. He is reaching down, ever down, toward a place of brightness, where He will once again emerge into the world. He holds His focus through the squeezing, eyes shut tightly, tiny fists clenched. She is pushing now, growling and squatting as sweat streams down into Her eyes. The women surround Her, holding Her up, offering encouragement. The people tire as the night wanes. They gather close around the fire, searching the sky for signs of the approaching dawn.

The crowning is next, a fiery pain that the Lady feels She cannot bear. She cries aloud, straining with all Her might. The baby God is moving, riding the waves of energy, willing Himself forward. At long last, the bright edge of the sun crests the trees. The people all stand and cheer, welcoming the brand-new light to the world. The Lady collapses, a triumphant smile on Her weary face. In the sudden silence that follows, the wail of a baby can be heard throughout the land.

Blessed Yule to you and yours!

Yule 2003: Book of Shadows

At this dark time of the year, I've been turning inward, contemplating the spiritual work that I've been doing over the past few seasons. A phrase that caught my inner eye recently is 'Book of Shadows.' Yes, I do have one and we all know the common definition of this type of tome: a sort of religious recipe book, a place to store the rituals and spells we have created, the lore we have learned, the thoughts we have about the spiritual work we've done. Some traditions pass down their own Book of Shadows, asking each initiate to copy it in their own handwriting, to help them integrate the wisdom within and to preserve their secret knowledge. Quester received a lovely blank Book of Shadows as a gift and he's capturing bits of wisdom that he plans to pass along to our children.

But I was thinking about the title itself, Book of Shadows. Why shadows? Why not a book of light? It reminds me of Plato's allegory of the cave: we are all, he says, prisoners in a cave, who have never seen the light of the outside world. The things that we think are real are only shadows, cast onto the wall of the cave by the light of the sun.

As human beings living on the physical plane, we cannot fully perceive things in their true forms. I do believe that we get glimpses of our own particular truths, yet when we bring them back into our everyday world, it is nearly impossible to explain them in words or even to fully express them in creative works of art. Yet we can remember that feeling of inner knowing, of understanding more than we did before.

Writing words in a physical Book of Shadows is one way to remind ourselves of the times when we have touched other realities and gone beyond our human selves, when we have been in intimate connection with the divine and the web of life. Other ways might be to include artwork in the Book of Shadows. But sometimes the memories of our altered states are triggered by other sensory reminders: the smell of the incense we used at our self-dedication, the sound that the wind in the pines made during our last ritual, the sensation of spinning when we sit in meditation, a bird call, the feel of the drum skin as we get into the rhythm.

I think that we have an inner Book of Shadows, a tome in the cosmic library that is the Akashic Records. Each person's Book is personalized by the experiences they've had, the work they've done, the people they've met and the places they've been. Also included are flavors of particularly memorable past (or future) lives and connections with patron deities or spirit guides. We can access this Book whenever we choose to do so, even if it may seem difficult when we're in traffic, meeting a deadline at work or trying to prepare food for hungry children while answering the phone and letting the cat out.

We can set up, quite deliberately, our own triggers (or, if you like, a Table of Contents). While meditating or in trance, select an image, affirmation or sensation that is particularly vivid for you. Concentrate on it and focus on letting it pervade your senses, for as long as feels right to you. Tell yourself that you can call on this symbol whenever you need to access your own inner wisdom. Then take the time to practice, as you would any skill. In moments when you don't feel particularly tense or stressed, mindfully call on your symbol and see where it takes you. Soon, you'll find yourself able to access your inner Book of Shadows when you most need to be reminded, such as on a difficult day or when you're sick or otherwise in crisis.

You can also have some fun with your physical-world Book of

Shadows. It's a great project for these long, cold winter days. Add sketches or a collage to its pages. Dab it with essential oils so it smells wonderful. Cover it with pieces of fabric with interesting textures. Add some sheet music. Write down your most outrageous and metaphoric dreams. Do your best to make it mirror (or 'shadow') your unfolding inner landscape and the inner Book of Shadows you are always creating. Enjoy and Blessed Be.

Yule 2005: What Do You Mean, 'Pagan Lent?'

A few years ago, Quester and I adopted the practice of doing a 'detox' fast between Samhain and Yule. Alcohol, refined sugar, caffeine, dairy products, masturbation, unhealthy communication: these are all things that have, at various times, been given up during this part of the Wheel, between the end of the old year and the rebirth of the sun.

Others in our coven have now begun to adopt this practice, too. Recently, some of us have chosen to add healthy things we'll do during this time period: practice daily yoga, do more divination, add an exercise routine. As I practiced this year's version (ahh, that daily yoga feels so delicious...), it came to me that what the endeavor is all about is purification and a test of the will.

Just as the Sun God waits in the womb of the Goddess, readying Himself for His rebirth as the tides of the year turn, so too do we wait in the Mother's womb. In the absence of the strong solar energy we have experienced through the spring and summer, we turn inward and contemplate where our journey has taken us. We let unneeded habits and distractions drop away and encourage methods that help us center and purify our spirits.

As modern people, most of us don't have to struggle to be sure we have enough food put aside for the long winter or endure the cold days and long bitter nights wondering if we'll be warm enough. We can retreat to a warm home and light our evenings with electricity. And so we are drawn to challenge ourselves in other ways. Giving up some of our 'creature comforts' and at the same time cleansing our bodies and energy systems of substances or thought patterns we wish to be rid of is just such a spiritual challenge, a test of the will. And at a time when celebrations and indulgences are in full swing, from the excess of the Thanksgiving feast to the treats of the Yule season, giving up sugar, alcohol or dairy products can be even more of a test.

In my experience, this purification challenge has great rewards. After a fairly brief time, I find myself feeling physically much clearer and emotionally more centered. My personal demon, refined sugar, has become easier to release over time. I don't indulge very often anymore. Aside from an occasional foray into chocolate or a homemade treat from Mom, I am able to calmly regard sugary food as a poison to my body and not feel tempted. This new mindset, I feel, is possible because of the 'sugar fast' I've done during the dark months over the past few years. And when I do choose to eat dessert, such as at Yule at the end of the fast, I can clearly see the results, feeling how it affects my body and my emotions.

The concept of adding to my personal practices during this time is relatively new. But it, too, feels like part of the purification. The challenge here is to add something healthy while integrating it as a balanced part of daily life. Most of us don't live a monastic lifestyle, so adding five hours of daily meditation probably isn't realistic. But 30 minutes, with a clear commitment to maintaining it, probably is. And over time, you'll notice how the new practice affects you. When Yule arrives, you may wish to keep this new practice or perhaps adjust the amount of time you're devoting to it.

Now, I realize I've just given you an idea that it is a bit too late to implement this year. But some people like to do this as we begin to approach spring, say from Imbolc to Ostara, sort of like a 'Pagan Lent.' Cleansing the body and the mind in preparation for the vibrant energy of spring, and testing the will as the sun ascends, can be just as powerful. Try it and you may be surprised by the results.

Yule 2006: Emotions and Change

Having conflicting feelings about change seems to be a universal human trait. Particularly around the winter holidays, we like traditions and 'doing things the way we've always done them.' Traditions and familiar ways are comforting, even if they no longer serve us. Even when we have initiated or created a change, sometimes it takes a while for our emotions to settle down. Since change is always going to be part of life, especially when we are pursuing spiritual growth, here are some ways to help yourself adjust.

Allow yourself to reminisce about the way things were before the change. Remember the positive things without trying to compare them to your new situation. When you talk about the past with others, try and do so with a smile, and without expressing regret or sorrow that things are different now.

Do something that you find comforting and relaxing. Get a massage, make a meal of your favorite foods or watch a funny movie. Be fully in the present moment while you are nurturing yourself. Let go of any negative thoughts or feelings that arise, giving yourself permission to relax and enjoy.

Acknowledge that change can be difficult and that you're going to need some time to integrate it into your life. This can be harder if you are the one who has created the change. 'I really wanted this job, so why is it taking me so long to get used to the new schedule and routine?' Try not to expect yourself to adapt immediately.

Find healthy ways to release your emotions. Write or draw in a journal, take a walk in the woods, shouting to the trees, or talk with a trusted friend. Vigorous exercise can also help; go for a run or play a game of basketball or freeze tag. Dance wildly to loud music in your kitchen. Do a ritual in which you release your fear or anger in the fire or candle flame. Release your feelings without blaming yourself or others for them.

The root of our strong feelings around change often has to do with fear of the unknown. This is true especially if the change isn't one that you initiated. But you can control how you react and adapt to the change. Coming up with a list of goals and a plan to achieve them can be helpful. Keep the goals realistic, with steps you can take right away. If you can't think of goals that will help you adjust, use divination to help focus your thoughts.

Establish new traditions, particularly ones that relate to this time of year. If you've recently moved to a new town or neighborhood, find a great hill and invite family or friends to come over for sledding. Invite some of your new neighbors over for hot chocolate and cookies on the afternoon of the Winter Solstice.

Make a list of blessings. Try listing seven blessings each day for a week. They can be as profound as being thankful for the unconditional love of your partner, or as seemingly simple as appreciating the sight of the bare-branched trees at dusk or the warm cup of tea you enjoyed that morning. Reread your lists, appreciating all the positive things in your life.

Celebrate the progress you've made. Especially if the change relates to your personal growth, give yourself credit for being proactive. It takes courage and boldness to step out of your comfort zone. Even if you're uncertain whether the change is what you wanted or expected, give yourself a pat on the back for trying something new.

Yule 2007: Self in Community

Over the past couple of years, I've been experiencing changes in my chosen spiritual community. I was involved in several active groups for a number of years, including being co-leader of the local SpiralScouts circle. These days, I'm doing less group ritual work and more solo and one-on-one magick. This goes along with how I'm pursuing my calling, which is focused on writing and other forms of creativity. It's like I'm returning to my roots as a solitary witch who reaches out to the community through the written word and individual contacts, as well as periodic networking with other Pagans.

Part of the process has been rethinking what it means to be in service to community. In the Pagan world, we often think of our clergy as leading covens, teaching classes, facilitating handfastings or doing interfaith outreach. These are all valid and necessary roles. Yet there are as many ways to serve one's community as there are people doing that work. Writing articles and books, creating websites and message boards, offering healing to an ill community member, taking care of a patch of land: these are just a few of the ways we may offer our help. Everyone and everything is interconnected, so any action we take that reaches out with helpful intentions has a ripple effect. The key is to offer part of yourself, with love, to another being.

In fact, community service is most effective when you're doing something you love to do, something that calls to your soul. We may look to the way others serve their community and in the process devalue our own gifts by taking them for granted. We hear about an acquaintance who volunteers at a hospice, reading to dying patients, and we think 'wow, that's so amazing. I could never do that; I'm just too sensitive.' We forget that every spring we go out and clean up trash and fallen branches as we walk our favorite trail. Yet our acquaintance might look on that task with admiration and even envy, because a knee injury limits her ability to hike. Each of us has unique gifts that we bring to all of our interactions in community.

We also constantly serve as role models for others, on many levels. As we move along our path, we not only model our actions and attitudes, but also energies and images on a more subtle level. Whether we know it or not, we are a beacon, shining our individual light into the universe. If we're doing a lot of solo introspective work, perhaps clearing our energy system of old patterns and healing our broken places, that work will show. Even if we've confided in no one but the Goddess, others will sense our positive energies and respond accordingly. On a subconscious level, they may be inspired to explore their own inner worlds or listen more carefully to what we have to say.

Pagans who have done work in covens, particularly if they started their journey in that setting, can feel set adrift when they find themselves doing much of their magick alone. They may feel that they lack a spiritual intimacy that they have felt when working with a group and can be unsure of how they fit into the greater Pagan community. Yet after all, we each are ultimately solitary practitioners, finding our own path of connection with the divine. As we connect with the universe, we realize that everything is connected; we are all part of the web of life. When you shovel your elderly neighbor's walk, you are doing community service. When you smile at a stranger or open the door for someone, you are reaching out and having positive effects beyond the moment.

When figuring out how to best serve your community, you might want to ponder these questions: What things do I most love to do? How can or do those things have a positive effect on others and the world? What are the ways that I already reach out to other beings? What does my heart say? Sit in a quiet place and ask yourself these questions, breathing deeply and opening your heart. Wait for answers to come to you or do some stream of consciousness writing on the subject. Before sleep, ask for information in the dream realm. You already know the answers, deep inside. It's just a matter of listening and then taking the actions that inspire you and feed your joy while fulfilling another's need or wish. It might just lead you in a wonderful new direction.

Vocation happens when our deep gladness meets the world's deep need.
Frederich Buechner

Yule 2008: Finding Magick Everywhere

One of my favorite holiday songs is 'The Christians and the Pagans' by singer-songwriter Dar Williams, written in the 1990s. If you haven't heard it and would like to, you can easily find it on the Internet. In the song, when explaining Paganism to a child being raised as a Christian, Jane says: 'You find magic from your God and we find magic everywhere.' Many Pagans believe that everything is sacred and, as such, we are constantly in the presence of the divine.

Yet how many of us get caught up in our daily activities, seeing our tasks as mundane or even stressful? How can we truly find magick in everything we do? At this busy time of year, when our inner senses may be telling us to slow down and turn inward, we often feel that we have a thousand things to do, on top of our usual list of activities.

It can help to stop and examine why we choose to do these things. Yes, it might be a tradition to send holiday cards and decorate your home, but dig deeper. Why do you want to give gifts to family and friends? At the root of these customs is the desire to show your love and caring for them. Perhaps you want to celebrate the return of the light as part of your spiritual connection with the seasons. Our ancestors reached out to their extended family and community at the dark time of year, knowing that together we are stronger and can help each other make it through the long winter. Concentrating on the positive reasons for our holiday preparations helps us bring joy to their accomplishment.

Aside from the added preparations for the Sabbat, we can also take a closer look at why we fill our days with certain activities. Meal preparation is necessary to fuel our bodies, so wouldn't it be nice to give it our focused attention and gratitude? Taking care of our homes provides us with a clean and comfortable place to spend time. The daily work we've chosen reflects our interests and our intentions. Taking time to exercise our bodies helps us feel physically and emotionally stronger. Our evening entertainment, whether from books or music or TV, helps spark our imagination and delight our senses. Rather than taking these things for granted, or even complaining about them, practice pausing and really noticing how we feel in each moment. Even when we notice things we'd like to change about our lives, we can work toward those changes without disparaging our current situation.

Where is the magick that surrounds you right now, in this moment? You're reading a Pagan text, absorbed by the words you read here. What room are you in? Is it warm or cold? Who is with you? How are the mysteries of the universe reflected in your surroundings? How do you feel? What is your energy level? By stopping periodically and asking yourself questions such as these, you can make it a habit to recognize the magick in everything.

When you continue to practice this focused awareness, you'll find that you're more open to the energies of the universe and its beings. You might receive insights or messages that help you along your path. Perhaps you'll be inspired to make positive changes or to show more appreciation for the life you've created. Even challenging situations can be affected by this practice. The winter blahs will fade away as you notice the sparkling snow outside your window or the deep indigo of the sky at dusk. The moon might speak to you of unexplored dreams. The poetry of a walk in the woods will call to you. A beloved work of art could spark your creativity. A friendly smile will create ripples of connection. Each breath you take will be a reminder of your divine nature. This holiday season, may you be blessed with magick everywhere.

Chapter 3

Imbolc

Imbolc, sometimes called Candlemas, celebrates the turning point from winter to spring. Here in New England, the nights are still long and the weather is cold, though the days grow longer and a bit lighter. It's the time when we plant the seeds of the spiritual work we want to pursue this year. We carefully craft our intentions, letting the growing light feed them as the Wheel begins to turn slowly toward spring. As part of our celebration, we make and bless the candles we'll use in this year's rituals. Our work at Imbolc might encompass setting new goals, releasing old patterns, creating healthy habits or planning new ways to become active in the Pagan community.

The early signs of spring appear: buds sprouting on the trees, snow beginning to melt and perhaps even a crocus or two coming up (though often we must wait for Spring Equinox for actual flowers). We are anxious for spring to arrive so we can once again take walks outside and work in the garden. Yet we still face wintry weather, such as snow, ice storms and chilly winds. We learn to be more patient, watching the slow progress of the land's awakening.

In Celtic lands, Imbolc was also known as Brighid's Day, honoring the Goddess of poetry, smithcraft and healing. We create crafts and poems and include them in our rituals. We have time to explore indoor pursuits such as learning about astrology, designing a garden or practicing martial arts. We may have the opportunity to help those who are in a crisis situation and need our healing energies. We explore ways to simplify our daily lives.

During the last few weeks of winter, burrowing under the icy surface to work with deeply felt emotions can be very powerful spiritual work. We can learn to flow with our own emotions and those of others. Imbolc is a good time to practice deep listening and pay closer attention to our inner landscape. We might find new ways to meditate, becoming more mindful or exploring our senses in more detail. As we shed light on our hidden depths, we watch the days grow gradually longer and warmer, lifting our spirits as the Wheel turns toward spring.

Imbolc 1997: Journeys to Create Reality: Walking

This is a tough time of year for me. One of my favorite activities for exercise, pleasure and spiritual balance is walking. The cold and icy weather makes a daily walk all but impossible and some weeks go by when I don't get out for a stroll at all.

Whether it is a brisk walk through the hilly city streets, a stroll in the woods or hiking in the mountains, walking is a magickal activity for Quester and I. When we first met, we went for long walks in the warm spring rain, usually at night ('Dancing under a streetlight in the rain is no fun alone.' – Quester), getting to know each other and sharing our hopes and dreams. The rhythm of our walking and breathing, talking and singing, became a ritual.

We still perform this ritual often, and over the years, we've discovered that the type of talking we do on our walks is different. It has a free and open quality to it, and the ideas and plans we come up with often manifest in our lives weeks and months, even years, later. Walking is what we choose to do when we need to feel more centered, individually or as a couple.

The energy pattern of the walk itself is a mini-ritual: a gradual buildup of energy, the release of intent and the return. Walking is a meditation, allowing us to enter the alpha state, conducive to working magick. We are part of our surroundings, yet also observers who move through them. We reaffirm our contact with the elements: the earth we tread, the air we breathe, the fire of the sun or moonlight, the water of rain or of the nearby lake, river or ocean. We envision our intentions and release them, our individual wills join with the creative energy of the Goddess. Then closing the circle, grounding once more where we began, yet changed in some way.

On our walks, Quester and I have worked to create our reality in many ways, using the spell to set goals, react to changes in our plans, solve problems or simply celebrate life. We create, refine and incorporate new ideas into our walks. Through application of this fun, practical magick ritual, we've changed jobs, found a new place to live, improved our physical health, found new outlets for our creativity and even added a new member to our family.

Soon it will be getting warmer and we'll step out and walk on a daily basis, energized and enlivened by this part of our magickal journey.

Imbolc 1998: Ice Storms

The recent ice storms have unquestionably affected beings throughout the state of Maine. However, I noticed that in the media the focus was almost exclusively on the effect on humans and our 'property.' If the effects of the heavy ice on the trees (who I would argue were the ones most hurt by it) were mentioned at all, it was only in the context of 'damage to property' or the fact that limbs fell on electric lines or houses. Animals and birds were only mentioned, to my knowledge, in the context of pets who may not have been welcomed in Red Cross shelters.

Now without a doubt we humans were inconvenienced by the storms, some much more severely than others. But as Pagans, I think we must look at the bigger picture.

I am no forestry expert by any means, but one perspective on the devastation to many trees is that it will make the forests healthier in the long run. The weaker trees would have been the first to fall, making way for younger, healthier trees, and trees of different varieties, to grow. Fallen trees will become homes for wildlife. Nature is adaptable, especially over long periods of time. The tree community will eventually be revitalized.

However, on an individual basis, consider the shock to the trees that lost limbs and perhaps life. Time runs much slower for long-lived trees than for humans, so from their perspective, the speed with which ice built up and broke or shattered the trees was like a lightning bolt. In the days after the storm, as I traveled around I could feel a sense of sadness mixed with disbelief from areas where many trees had been hurt and killed. It will no doubt take months or years before many of the survivors will return to their usual way of being.

Animals and birds were, if anything, more affected by the ice than humans. Those without caves or burrows, such as herds of deer, must be having a really hard time finding shelter. Food was (and is) hard to come by when a thick impenetrable layer of ice covers the ground and trees. Birds were cold and wet, and many surely died as a result of the ice storms. Again, taking a long-term view, one can argue that species of animals will thrive as a result of their diminished numbers, and the ice storms are certainly a phenomenon of nature. But I have a hard time getting beyond the sorrow I feel for the individual creatures in their pain and suffering to truly embrace this view.

One reason that our selfishness in describing how the crisis affected Maine as a whole disturbs me is the cause of our shifts in weather. Having lived in Maine my whole life, I have noticed changes in our weather patterns. I believe global warming due to our pollution of the ecosystem plays a large part in the changes taking place. We shouldn't be so surprised and almost insulted by what comes of it. Karma, anyone? Of course, if as a society we're ignorant and selfish enough to pollute our home to this extent and then deny it, I shouldn't be surprised that we focus on our own survival to the exclusion of other equally valid life forms.

Speaking of other life forms, I wonder how the nature spirits were affected by the recent weather. No doubt there were ice faeries frolicking in joy, for the ice was very beautiful even in its destruction. But what about dryads who lost their homes? (I must mention here, with this talk of homeless tree nymphs, an excellent and hilarious novel that Quester and I just read. If you haven't read *Tex and Molly in the Afterlife* by Maine writer Richard Grant, you should!)

I guess it will take time to examine the changes made and damage done. In the spring, as we are able to hike out into the woods, we can see and feel for ourselves how the extreme weather has affected the greater reality around us.

Imbolc 2000: Wicca and Astrology: A Book Review

I just finished reading a book that I found to be an excellent source of ideas, as well as a great read. *The Witch's Circle* by Maria Kay Simms is a general introduction to Wicca, as well as a handbook for integrating elements of astrology into your Sabbats and Esbats.

The author, known as Lady Mari to her coven, Circle of the Cosmic Muse, was an astrologer for many years before coming to Wicca. She was trained in what she refers to as the 'West Coast eclectic' tradition. The book begins with an exploration of astrological ages. She contends that despite the focus on the age of Aquarius, we are still very much in the age of Pisces, and she sees the current spiritual renaissance as a move towards the more positive aspects of Pisces, including a synthesis with its opposite sign, Virgo. Next is Mari's overview of neo-Paganism and Wicca, including a well-written section on ethics. Her view of the subject is refreshing and interesting reading, even for those who have read many such introductory texts. She includes a discussion of being 'out of the broom closet,' and the pros and cons of using 'the W word' (witch).

Lady Mari has drawn on her extensive knowledge of astrology to create a balanced and intriguing system of rituals. Her unique look at the Wheel of the Year and her synthesis of the movement of the sun and moon through the signs of the zodiac, in my opinion, would be of interest to many Pagans.

The premise is simple: at each month's Full Moon, the moon is in the opposite sign of the zodiac from the sun. This is common sense, once you think about it. The reason the moon appears full is that it is directly opposite the sun, reflecting all of the sun's light. The complementary and opposing aspects of the two signs are illustrated within each ritual, in order to shed light on our own lives.

A sample ritual is given for each Esbat. The format is the same for each one, merging the astrological elements with more traditional Wicca.

A short dialogue between the Sun (God) and the Moon (Goddess) role-plays the two signs and leads into the Charge of the Goddess, in which Her special perspective on the season, from the viewpoint of the opposite sign, provides the complement and balance. This, then, provides the theme and lead-in for the special participatory working for the group (139-140).

The Esbats are connected with the seasons of the year and the cycle of birth, death and rebirth.

In this system, the Sabbats are also linked with the phases of the moon. As we navigate the Wheel of the Year, we go through similar phases to those the moon travels through each month. Lady Mari has connected each of the eight Wiccan Sabbats with a corresponding lunar phase, which describes the energy of that time of year. She uses the four standard lunar phases and also the more obscure cross-quarter phases of the moon, which she attributes to astrologer-philosopher Dane Rudhyar. The Winter Solstice is the new moon phase of the year, with its new beginnings, followed by Imbolc, which is the crescent, then the Spring Equinox, with its first quarter energies. Beltane is the gibbous or waxing time of year, followed by the Summer Solstice as Full Moon, when the sun is at its peak of power. Lughnasadh is the disseminating phase, Fall Equinox would be last quarter and Samhain relates to the Balsamic (waning) moon, with the focus on death and the seeds of rebirth. If this brief explanation seems confusing, rest assured that the chapter on 'Astrology and Ritual' is easy to absorb, with charts included to aid visual learners.

The only drawback I found in the book is that the rituals are a bit too elaborate. The speeches are long and flowery, which in my experience can be dull or distracting. But later in the book Lady Mari does explain that while these rituals are given as examples of her coven's tradition, they are often improvised within the form given. She writes,

> We have, for the most part, quit writing our Moons. Instead, we talk over the basic symbolism of the sign polarities and any issues that we think might be particularly relevant to our group, decide on something to do for the working, and then we 'wing it' (235).

I know a couple of Pagan astrologers and most of us at least dabble a bit, referring to people by their sun signs and reading our daily horoscope. But this book goes beyond 'pop astrology.' Within our rituals of worship, the system described here can help us to grow spiritually and attune to the cycles of the earth and the solar system. I think this book with its wealth of ideas would be an excellent addition to the library of any Pagan, no matter your astrological sign or tradition.

Imbolc 2001: Patterns

I've been working a lot on patterns lately. It is somewhat of a New Age cliché by now, this talk of 'getting rid of old patterns' that hold you back from becoming a whole and healthy person. I find the metaphor is useful and it has at least a kernel of truth in it. But as with many such things, to look deeper and to turn the concept on its head can yield a more meaningful tool for growth.

Think about it: what chronic unpleasant behavior or emotion do you have that you could consider an 'old pattern?' Have you tried to get rid of this behavior, only to have it recur in the most unexpected of ways? Most of us have at least one. Perhaps it's low self-esteem, being a martyr or feeling superior to others. Maybe it's overeating, smoking or even something as simple as drinking too much coffee. If it bothers you and you want to get rid of it, but find yourself struggling to do so, it's a pattern.

As I work to get rid of some of my own persistent patterns, I've been wondering why the word is associated with a negative behavior or series of thoughts. Aren't we all part of the web of life? Isn't that a pattern on the grandest, most positive scale? Maybe instead of just cleaning the cobwebs out of my own little corner of the world, I also need to spin a sparkling new section of the web.

Imbolc is an ideal time to come up with some new and vibrant patterns for your life. Here in the northeast United States, we're still in the middle of winter; we cannot yet plant seeds for the spring to come. But we can design our gardens. We can begin to dream of the projects and goals we will sow.

All that which we shed from Samhain to Yule has been composted, leaving us stripped bare, purified and ready for Brighid's fiery inspiration. As you practice your Craft this season, consider the pattern on which this lifetime is based. What are your unique talents and gifts? How can you share those talents and use them to contribute to the weaving of the universe? Think of the things that bring you joy and infectious delight that is easily and blissfully shared with others.

Now get into brainstorming mode. Make a list of goals, including anything that strikes your fancy, whether abstract or concrete. Try not to let your 'old patterns' get in the way. You can do anything: learn to dance or play the flute; write a book; get your degree; build your own Stonehenge; embrace peace; find your true love. Don't add things that you think you 'should' do. Creating a new pattern or reweaving a section that you had forgotten about requires a spark of interest and curiosity. Look to your muse or ask Brighid for her aid.

Now weave this positive magick into your self-improvement work. When an 'old pattern' threatens to bring you down, set it deliberately aside. Pick up your loom and work on your exciting new section of the web. Smile, knowing that you are doing something you truly love to do and that you are an integral part of the patterns of the web of life.

Imbolc 2002: Listening

Imbolc is a good time of the year for listening. The nights are still long and cold, even though the days grow longer and a bit lighter. If you practice deep listening, you can hear the tiny seed of pure potential that wakens beneath the surface.

I don't simply mean listening more carefully to your friends and family, although that is a skill worth nurturing. I don't even mean observing quietly the changes going on underneath the snow and frozen ground, which can be a valid way to tune in to the season's turning point. What I refer to is cultivating inner stillness, so you can sense the motion within that will lead to a new idea or vision. Listen for the whispers of the divine in your psyche, leading you to a new awakening.

An article I read recently on intuition had the usual recommendations about writing down your dreams, noticing synchronicity and being open to sudden 'gut feelings.' But a main emphasis was on being quiet and still for at least a few minutes each day, to allow regular time without outside stimuli so that the quiet voice of your inner knowing can be heard. Many of us have busy days and evenings. But this time of the winter, when the weather reinforces our natural inclination to hibernate, is a good time to begin to allow ourselves a brief respite of silence each day.

Create sacred space for yourself in a way that feels natural and good. Sit or lie in a comfortable position and, at first, simply focus on your breathing. Some people find meditation difficult because they strive to 'empty the mind,' and then get frustrated when thoughts continue to arise. Instead, realize that thinking is what the brain is trained to do. Let it continue to do its job, but instead of clinging to or pushing away each thought, simply let them flow through you like water in a stream. Note calmly the natural pauses that begin to stretch out between the thoughts. Within this flowing of silence and ideas, you can perhaps glimpse a silvery flash, a jewel-like trout that is a kernel of truth.

Like any skill, this deep listening gets easier with practice. Good times for listening are in the morning, before your day has fully begun; in bed before sleeping, when your quiet expectancy can meld into your dreams; or on a walk in the snow, when the normal sounds of nature or city become muffled and the landscape is magickally transformed.

Once your practice of listening has brought you ideas, or seeds of ideas, you can begin working with them magickally. Perhaps they will provide inspiration for your creative projects. Or if you work with goals at Imbolc, you can phrase them as such. You can create affirmations for yourself around what has been revealed to you or use the ideas to form questions for further exploration in dreams or trance. It is also important to give thanks for these inner treasures.

Whatever you decide to do with the things you hear when listening within, the practice itself can be valuable. Take some time to listen, this Imbolc time, and chances are you'll be rewarded richly with the stirring of seeds deep inside, ready to be planted as the Wheel turns toward spring.

Imbolc 2003: Beneath the Surface

At this time of the year, the water that we see around us is, for the most part, frozen. Snow and ice make up the landscape and below that lies the frozen ground. Once in a while we may have a hint of the thaw to come, when puddles develop on the driveway or icicles drip on a warm afternoon. But for the most part, all appears to be still. Yet water continues to move under the surface, deep under the ground, flowing where it can't be seen.

In modern society, it is often the same with the emotions we experience. We go to work, we shop at the grocery store, we smile at our neighbors and, when they ask, say that we are 'fine.' Yet under the surface layer of polite civility, we all experience a wide range of emotions. We are also affected by the emotions of the people around us, whether or not we acknowledge it consciously.

How do we, as Pagan priests and priestesses, deal with our own emotions and with the tides of others' feelings? Our basic magickal training usually deals with how to work with emotions. Yet I find that even after years of practice, it is helpful to purposefully engage oneself on an emotional level and find new ways of opening to the lessons of the watery realm. For me, the image of flow is very helpful when learning to better harness the power of emotions.

Emotions, like water, tend to flow into the path of least resistance and tend to follow the same patterns over and over. Getting rid of our old patterns of emotions, or unhealthy ways of coping with them, can be difficult even when we are ready to release them. These emotions, or our habitual reactions to them, can become stuck in the body and can manifest as symptoms of illness or discomfort.

In order to get rid of these blockages and help find new channels for one's emotions, I recommend learning a new physical skill and practicing it regularly. Whether it's yoga, tai chi, skiing, juggling or learning new dance steps, moving your body in a new way on a regular basis helps it to reset and recharge. Exercise also helps us release stress, which may build up as we work on banishing outworn or difficult emotional patterns.

Another important tool is taking the time to notice how your body reacts when you feel various emotions. Where is the seat of your anger? What happens in your chest when you feel sad? Is your joy coated with a golden yellow color? Once you've identified these sensations, when you encounter them in daily life you can consciously breathe into them, allowing any blockages to release. When I notice these patterned responses in my body, I slow my breathing and form an image of the emotion, allowing its energy to flow out like water. I visualize it flowing out at the back of my neck and down my back like a waterfall, to fall harmlessly to the ground where it is reabsorbed.

Of course, some of the emotions we experience might not be our own. Many of us who are drawn to spiritual work are empaths, people who are especially sensitive to energies, partic ularly emotions. When we begin our magickal training, ideally we learn basic skills to protect ourselves from unwanted energies. We learn to recognize when the emotions we are experiencing are not our own and can then ground them appro- priately. Basic techniques of breathing and meditation can help in situations when we are sensitive to the emotions around us.

However, even if we've been dealing with our empathy and sensitivity for many years, there are situations when it can overwhelm us. It's often challenging to effectively stay centered when affected by the emotions of those closest to us: our partner or spouse, child, close friend or roommate. Those who live with us have a particularly strong effect, since emotional energies remain in the home and can collect like dust.

What are some tools that can help in these situations? When a loved one is dealing with volatile emotions, if they are receptive to it you can teach them how to breathe and ground themselves. Be sure to cleanse your home regularly, which means basic physical cleaning, followed by simple energy cleansing techniques such as sprinkling salt water, smudging with sage or incense or drumming and toning until the energies are clearer (which you can often feel, if not see). You can help your loved one create an altar or shrine to focus and release strong feelings, or if the person is not receptive to that idea, you can charge an item to help you deal with the strong emotions surrounding you and place it on your own altar.

When we are closely involved with a loved one in an emotional crisis, like an argument, it can be even more challenging to stay centered. Being able to take a few moments to rest outside the pattern of the conflict can be helpful. Breathe and center yourself, then step back from your own feelings about the situation and deliberately try to experience what the other person is feeling. Then step back again, moving away from that set of emotions. If you need to, take a break and agree to continue the conversation later.

When you return to the discussion, try and source the person as they express themselves as clearly as they can. Sourcing involves letting divine energy manifest through you and directing it at the recipient. It is important not to use your own energy for this, but instead to let the energy of the Goddess or God flow through your body. Listen to your loved one with your entire being. Don't try to analyze or rationalize their feelings, but do acknowledge and respect them. If the two of you are willing to do spiritual work together, have them practice these same techniques with you. This is undoubtedly quite challenging work, but can also be very rewarding.

As we hibernate through these frozen weeks of winter, burrowing under the surface to work with our deeply felt emotions, alone or with others, can be very powerful spiritual work. And when the thawing time arrives, we can greet spring freshly energized and feeling healthy. Our emotions will flow like a spring stream and we can take time to sit on the bank, marveling at the lessons we learn from them.

Imbolc 2004: Healing in a Crisis

Late in December, my mother was in a serious car accident. As I write, thanks in part to the technological marvels of modern Western medicine, she's alive and stable, though not 'out of the woods' yet. It is an unfortunate fact that, sooner or later, most of us will be in a situation when someone we love is in intensive care. How can we best add our magick, healing and blessings to the necessary treatments and care our loved one is receiving? How can we do so while working within the restrictions placed on us by the hospital? And how can we do the greatest good for our loved one while not depleting our own energy resources? Here are a few things I've recently discovered.

- **Protect yourself.** Being in the hospital even as a visitor is stressful, particularly if you're an empath. My friend who is a nurse advises that what works for her is to surround herself in a sphere of light and repeat a mantra such as 'I allow in only the highest good and radiate out only the highest good.'
- **Surround your loved one in a sphere of light.** Set up a sphere around their bed, which is permeable to medical personnel and procedures, yet serves to focus any healing energies being sent. If other family members or friends are sending healing energy, let them know what you've done so they can add the sphere to their visualizations. Reinforce the sphere each day.
- **Talk to your loved one**, either aloud or silently, even if they are unconscious. Even if asleep or sedated, they may be able to hear you on some level. Be positive and encouraging and tell them you love them.
- **Touch your loved one.** Even if you can only reach his or her hand or foot, there is powerful healing in simple loving touch. If you know Reiki or some other form of hands-on healing, all the better.

- **Be kind to the medical staff.** Even under extreme stress, treat other people as you'd want to be treated. They work hard to do their best for every patient. If they ask you to leave the room, do so promptly and let them do their work. You can still do healing for your loved one from the waiting room. I've found that some of the nurses know about Reiki and they tend to work around me when I'm doing it. I think they are willing to do that because I've been so willing to get out of their way whenever I'm asked.
- **Cry.** Crying is a good way to relieve stress and keep yourself centered. It's worse for you to keep your emotions inside. If you don't want to cry in front of others, such as in a waiting room, take a short walk or just cry in the restroom.
- **If you can, leave a picture**, a special rock, shell or a stuffed animal in the person's room. Even in the intensive care unit, you can often leave a small item on the windowsill. If that's not possible, make sure you have an item representing the person on your altar (a good idea anyway). Or wear something that reminds you of your loved one. I have a faerie pin that Mom gave me, which I'm wearing each day. The item will help you maintain a strong connection to your loved one even when you can't be there in person.
- **Accept support** from the community. Support and energy of all types is welcome, even if it is not Pagan. My Mom is not Christian, yet she's got several church groups praying for her (they've been asked to do so by other friends and family members). We all ultimately worship the same divine, no matter which names we give it. Encourage all energies sent with positive intent to help the healing process.
- **Accept your limitations.** The hardest lesson to learn is that, despite all your love and wishes, it is really the choice of your loved one whether to live or die, and when and how

fast to heal. You must accept that choice and give the person your full support. Yes, you can pray for the best and do magick for healing, but ultimately they must do as they wish with that energy. Wouldn't you want the same freedom if you were in a similar situation? The individual's soul must make the choice.

I truly hope that you'll never need to use any of this advice. May you and your family and friends be well and have a blessed Imbolc.

Imbolc 2006: Paying Attention

It is Imbolc, the time when we plant the seeds of the spiritual work we want to pursue this year. We pledge our goals and intents, letting the growing light feed them as the Wheel begins to turn slowly toward spring. But what about the step that comes before that pledge? How do we know what our goals should be? How do we decide where to focus our magick?

To some people, those questions will be moot. The focus is obvious: if you are feeling ill, your intent will be to heal; if you're looking for a new job or home, you'll want to put your energy behind that process. But for others, it may not be so crystal-clear. Perhaps you're feeling uninspired and not sure what to focus on. Or maybe there are so many exciting possibilities that you're having trouble choosing. A simple-sounding yet profound technique may be just the tool you need: mindfulness meditation. Or, even more simply put: paying attention.

Mindfulness meditation is an ancient Buddhist practice. Depending on where you learn it, there are certain techniques and ways of practicing. What I'm talking about here, though, is the art of being in the moment, of paying careful attention as you go through daily life. No matter what you are doing, the idea is to stay present, rather than allowing your thoughts to dwell in the past or speculate about the future.

In his book *Wherever You Go There You Are: Mindfulness Meditation in Everyday Life,* Jon Kabat-Zinn describes mindfulness as 'the art of conscious living.' He goes on,

> Mindfulness means paying attention in a particular way: on purpose, in the present moment and nonjudgmentally. This kind of attention nurtures greater awareness, clarity and acceptance of present-moment reality. It wakes us up to the fact that our lives unfold only in moments. If we are not fully present for many of those moments, we may not only miss what is most valuable in our lives but also fail to realize the richness and the depth of our possibilities for growth and transformation (4).

You may wonder about the seeming paradox between 'being with what is' and actively practicing magick (often defined as 'the art of changing consciousness at will'). However, used as a tool, mindfulness meditation can provide clues about potential goals. You can then pursue those goals with a clear, strong intent, consciously choosing the best path for your future growth.

There are various ways these clues might arise. First, as you practice being in the moment, you'll notice that it is sometimes difficult and at other times easy. Ask yourself: 'What is it difficult for me to be here for?' 'What activities or places cause me joy and ease in the moment?' Explore the emotions that arise, not judging them, but noticing what they are and what situations seem to trigger them. You may find some new insights into areas you want to explore.

Second, as you clear your mind, you may begin to notice things you would have once overlooked. Augury, or the art of divination by the observation of natural phenomena, can bring you personalized information. For example, seeing a deer break away from the herd and leap joyfully over a fallen log might spark a thought in you about a new approach to a troubled relationship. You can then form that crystallized awareness into a resolution for your work this year.

In a similar vein, you might begin to notice moments of synchronicity that point you toward your goals. Perhaps you've been thinking of going back to college, but you don't quite know what you want to study. A friend happens to mention an article she read about Native American artifacts being unearthed in Vermont and the next day you see an ad for a nearby college that mentions their acclaimed archaeology program. You remember that when you were in elementary school, that was what you wanted to do when you grew up. Aha! Suddenly you're excited about this new path. Opening and clearing your mind can allow long-held desires to rise to the surface.

The ideas and insights that come up for you while practicing mindfulness will be uniquely yours. You can then mold them into a magickal intent to plant at Imbolc and concrete actions to take throughout the year. Who knows, you may even find that the further practice of mindfulness itself becomes a goal! May you find and plant the seeds that are just right for your own spiritual garden. Blessed Imbolc!

Imbolc 2007: Unlocking Your Faerie Senses

As children, we learn about the five senses and how they work. As we pursue our magick, we become aware of our 'sixth sense' and perhaps of other inner senses. But have you ever experimented with your five basic senses? You can expand them until you experience the everyday world in a new way, as the faeries do.

If you'd like to try it, find a time when you can relax and be undisturbed. Ground and center yourself and do some deep breathing (but don't fall asleep). Pick a sense and focus on it fully. Allow your awareness to expand, going into a light trance state. Explore the sense in a relaxed and joyful way. Here are some ideas to get you started. Most importantly: have fun!

- **Sight.** Faerie sight is much like seeing auras. Everything has an energy field surrounding it and, with practice, you can 'see' the swirling lights and colors. Each person experiences this in a different way: you may literally see the auras, you may feel or intuit the energy they emit or perhaps the normal colors of the world become more bright and vivid. Start by allowing your eyes to go slightly out of focus. Be sure to continue breathing slowly as you look around. It helps to practice this exercise outside in a setting of natural beauty. See the trees as they breathe and communicate with one another. Watch the energy of moving water. Shut your eyes and notice how you can still use your faerie sight. At night, notice the unique color of each star or watch the flames of a fire as they dance.

- **Hearing.** The obvious thing to do when exploring sound is to listen to music. Sit in a dark room and concentrate all your attention on the music you have chosen, preferably something complex and many-layered. Let your imagination flow, perhaps adding images or colors to the sounds. Another way to explore faerie hearing is to take a silent hike. It works best if you hike with another person, agreeing to remain silent. As you walk quietly, you'll notice sounds that otherwise would have stayed in the background. You have the option of conversing with your companion but you have chosen not to, and this contrast will allow you to focus even more fully on the sounds around you.

- **Touch.** Everything we touch has a unique texture, but most of us go through daily life not noticing. Devote an hour to really focusing on the feel of each item you touch. Explore the contrast between the textures and temperatures of the things around you. Each time you touch yourself or another person, do so with intention and love. Use gentle touch to communicate your feelings to your loved ones.

Remember that touch is not only experienced through your hands: pay attention to how your clothes feel as they touch your skin, intentionally rub your face against your cat's soft fur or notice as you shower or bathe how the water feels on all your surfaces.

- **Taste.** There are several things you can do to enhance your sense of taste. One is to really focus on the food you are eating. Eat slowly, savouring each morsel. Often when we eat outdoors, while hiking or camping, it seems that even the simplest foods are more flavorful and satisfying. Try eating outdoors during a winter hike. Or surround yourself with beauty as you eat, lighting candles and adding a plant or some flowers to your table. Often the fey sense of taste is expanded by trying unusual combinations of foods.

- **Smell.** The sense of smell is strongly connected to memory. Have you ever smelled something and immediately been transported to a certain place and time from your past? Think about the scents that you like the most and the memories they connect with. Collect several strong-smelling items and then close your eyes and breathe them in deeply, one at a time. Notice smells as you go about your day and allow yourself to take a few moments to fully appreciate them. If you smell something strong, don't immediately label it as either a 'bad' or 'good' smell. Instead, notice its nuances and how the scent fluctuates.

As you practice working with your faerie senses, you'll notice that you begin to use them more regularly, as a natural part of life. You can combine them by fully eating a meal with your senses of smell and taste open or enjoying the feel and sound of pencil on paper as you work on a sketch or do some writing. Take a hike or walk where your intent is to open all of your senses fully. Host a Faerie Feast for your coven or group of friends. Enjoy the pleasures of existing in a physical body created to interact with the world. Blessed Be!

Imbolc 2008: President Who?

I know you've been hearing a lot about the Presidential election lately. It's been all over the media. You're probably amazed at how an independent write-in candidate could be unanimously elected to the helm of the EarthTides Pagan Network – wait, what did you think we were talking about?! Kidding aside, I'm excited to be helping lead and serve this cool statewide organization that I've been part of for many years now.

What's my platform? Well, there isn't one, really, but here I'll offer some goals and thoughts. I want to help us continue to fulfill the EarthTides mission. I want to encourage and implement new ideas for connection and education, and for supporting each other in our practices. I plan to continue sharing my thoughts in this column and on the Internet. I'd love to hear your wants and needs about EPN. And I'm going to finally make it to the Common Ground Fair to work a shift at the booth!

It seems that being Pagan often goes hand-in-hand with other aspects of living an alternative lifestyle. Because of our beliefs, many of us are also interested in simpler living, environmentalism, vegetarianism and veganism, homeschooling, role-playing games, historical re-enactment, polyamory, political activism, human and animal rights and/or various other non-mainstream pursuits and ways of living. Because of a growing awareness of the issues and problems created by the modern industrial way of life, some of these notions are becoming familiar to more people. This includes the growth of awareness and acceptance of Paganism over the past decade.

Perhaps the most noticeable recent change, though, is in the area of environmentalism and simpler living. Because of the publicity that climate change is receiving in the mainstream media, it seems that many people are talking about how to reduce their personal impact on the environment. There are now a myriad of websites and blogs devoted to sharing ideas for simpler living, many of which will be familiar to Pagans who have been choosing these options for years (from bringing your own dishes to potlucks rather than using paper plates, to hanging out clothes instead of using a dryer, to shopping for clothing at thrift stores and the like). It seems that Mother Earth is making her needs known in wider and wider circles, as more people 'go green.'

How can we, as Pagans who have reverence for the earth, encourage this awakening? How does education about environmentalism and the actions we can each take fit with education and outreach about Paganism as a whole? How can we offer our help? I think a discussion of the intersection of Pagan values and the changes taking place in the wider culture would be of value to us at this time. As Pagans, we can reach out and use our connection with the earth to help conserve wilderness areas, preserve resources and also to help others find the joy and satisfaction that come from living lightly on the planet.

In addition, the needs of Maine's Pagan community are changing as we grow. It was once a challenge just to locate other Pagans with whom to network, and it still is in some areas. Yet we're now at a point where events like Popham Beach Beltane and Pagan Pride Day, and the popularity of the EPN booth at the Common Ground Fair, illustrate what a vibrant community we have. How can EarthTides adjust to better serve the diverse needs of today's Pagans? How can we improve the network of connections? What types of education can we offer to those who have been on the path for quite some time? What types of programs or services could EarthTides offer to you and your family or coven? Think about not only what you'd like to receive, but also what you might have to offer.

I'm very interested in hearing your feedback about EarthTides and how we best can support you and other Pagans in Maine and beyond. Please send along your feedback and new ideas.

Imbolc 2009: A Simpler Way

Many of us lead complex modern lifestyles. Even if we've incorporated some back-to-the-land ideas, we still have to cope with the fast pace of our culture. The mental list of things we 'need' to accomplish each day can seem endless. In the depths of winter, perhaps we can take some time to deliberately simplify our lives. This will help us create more space, more quiet in which to listen to the voices of the deities, the universe or our own inner selves.

When our days are constantly cluttered with noise and bustling activity, it's hard to remain centered. Even when we set aside time for meditation or contemplation, it can take a while to release the layers of chatter and buzz. If you're feeling drawn to a simpler way of being, here are some steps you can take in order to slow down and enjoy the moment:

- **Consolidate your computer time.** Between e-mail, Facebook, blogs and other forms of online communication, you can spend much of your day reacting to what's happening on the screen. Set aside 30 to 60 minutes each day to stay current with your personal communication. Then step away from the computer and turn your attention to your other priorities.
- **Turn off the TV and the radio.** The news can be interesting and music is pleasant, but what's it like hearing the natural sounds around you and letting your own thoughts be your soundtrack? Taking a few days each week to shut off these electronic noises won't leave you out of the loop. The news cycle is like a soap opera; it's easy to catch up with the plot after you've missed a few episodes.
- **Eat simple meals.** For breakfast, how about a banana and some freshly-squeezed orange juice? Yep, that's it. If you're

hungry an hour or two later, eat a handful of almonds. We can get carried away with elaborate or over-processed foods, when our bodies would be just as happy (and perhaps happier) with something basic yet delicious. Sure, you might get hungry more often, but grazing on healthy snacks is good for you.

- **Spend time with a very young child.** Toddlers have a marvelously uncomplicated world. They play with what's in front of them and don't worry about what's coming next unless they're ready for a change. Borrow a child from a friend or relative for an hour or two. Sit down on the floor with him and build block towers. You'll soon be grounded in the moment and the child's parents will thank you for a bit of time to themselves. If you don't know any little ones, find an energetic dog to play with. She'll adore you for throwing the ball 72 times in a row. Be present.

- **Do one thing at a time.** With so much on the 'to do' list, it's tempting to multi-task. Instead, give each task your undivided attention until it's done or until you come to a natural stopping point. Start or finish projects you've been procrastinating about. It'll feel so great to cross it off the list, knowing you've done your best. And then you can move on to more pleasant activities or take a break and do nothing at all.

- **Sleep in.** Even on the weekends, many people force themselves out of bed before they're fully rested. Sleep until you're truly done. Then stretch leisurely, snuggle your partner or do some deep breathing. Avoid scheduling morning appointments. Rest is important. You're not being lazy, you're recharging.

- **Do a simple ritual.** Cast a circle and then open yourself to the energies of the cosmos. Just sit quietly and listen, without reaching for a wand, athame, cauldron or other tool. Let your working unfold spontaneously. To raise energy, perhaps create and repeat a simple chant. Enjoy being alone in your private sacred space.

- **Stay home more often.** If you don't already have one, make a special spot for yourself in your home. It should be relaxing and comfortable, perhaps situated by a window or your altar. Experience the peace of just sitting and relaxing. Enjoy a simple pastime like knitting, doing a crossword puzzle or reading a novel. For a whole evening, do something that isn't at all 'productive.' The to-do list will wait.

- **Avoid 'helium hand.'** I have a friend, a single parent who, whenever a group asks for a volunteer, watches her hand go up automatically. She soon becomes overwhelmed by the amount of work on her plate. Volunteering is wonderful, but do it with an awareness of how much time you actually have available to give. Not only will this help you keep your life simpler, but also the volunteer jobs you do choose to focus on will receive your full attention. Give quality, not necessarily quantity.

If you reflect on your life and the things you choose to do, you'll be able to find other ways to simplify. Make a list. If an activity feels like a burden or creates complications you'd be better off without, find a way to release or change it. Over the years, we add new interests and pursuits to our lives. Yet we often forget to make room for them by letting go of other tasks and hobbies. By looking carefully at your list and noticing how you feel about each item, you'll be well on your way to crafting a simpler, more enjoyable life.

Chapter 4

Ostara

At the Vernal Equinox, the days and nights are of equal length, poised on the edge of a turn towards greater solar light and energy. Pagans celebrate Ostara, also known as Eostar. As the Wheel turns, we continue our steady progress toward the goals we set at Yule or Imbolc. Even in the darkest part of winter, we knew that the earth would grow green once again. We are empowered by the faith that, like the plants who await the sun's warmth, we'll be provided for physically, mentally and spiritually.

Spring has arrived at last and we can begin to plant some of the hardier crops. We put our plans in motion, getting outdoors more and perhaps taking a road trip. We're more inclined to venture out to social gatherings and our Ostara rituals are often full of singing and dancing. Like the earth's other creatures, we feel playful and full of energy.

The precise balance of light and dark at the Spring Equinox can inspire us to bring more balance into our own lives. A period of cleansing might be in order, to brush away the cobwebs of winter. Spring is a fertile time, when we allow new aspects of ourselves to flourish. It's time to nurture the seeds we planted at Imbolc, tending to our spiritual gardens as well as our physical ones. We may try different spiritual practices, tell our stories or delve into new philosophies.

At Ostara the days and nights are often rainy. Water is symbolic of the subconscious realms. Like the rain and snowmelt which fill the rivers and streams, our emotions rush through us with abandon. We can learn to honor the lessons they have for us. By going with the flow and letting go of the need to control each moment of our journey, we instead allow life to unfold in all its beauty.

Ostara 1997: Journeys to Create Reality: The Road Trip

I've written before about walking as a ritual. Another type of magickal journey Quester and I enjoy is our annual vacation. We combine a camping trip with a day at a music festival and perhaps a night out in a small city. We usually travel in New England or upstate New York; the White Mountains of New Hampshire are one of our favorite spots. These road trips, which we jokingly call our shamanic journeys, contain unexpected delights and moments of synchronicity. They also help us put our plans for the future into motion.

There's something magickal about hurtling your consciousness over vast distances at high speed and coming to rest in a new place. Just imagine what our ancient ancestors would have thought of a car ride! We have sought and found many places of power in our travels, from waterfalls to mountaintops to weathered covered bridges. Teachers have come into our lives and quickly gone again, like the witch in her broken-down purple microbus in Vermont, kind strangers who shared a delicious meal with us at a rest stop and a determined through-hiker on the last leg of his Appalachian trail trek. One morning we woke up to discover that a dear old friend, whom we hadn't seen or talked with for years, was camped in the site across from us. Is this type of synchronicity more frequent on vacation or do we just have more time to notice it?

During our journey, time opens up. We are removed from our usual daily routines and concerns, so we can focus on each other and our future plans. We dwell closer to the 'between-time.' Rituals done on vacation take on added significance, too. I'm still filled with wonder when I remember one powerful ritual we did in a nearly deserted campground, with the full moon rising over the lake. We are less concerned with the details of a ritual, which allows for more spontaneity. Living outdoors in the elements puts us more closely in tune with the earth's energy patterns. I tend to have more active and significant dreams during our journeys.

On vacation, we take time to play at creating our reality. We are open to new ideas and possibilities, even ones that might seem silly or far-out. We pause at this point on our life's path and examine the many off-shoots of the main trail. We consider all of the probable ways we could go, even hiking off into the woods or climbing a tree! During one of our trips we decided how I would get out of a bad situation at work. Despite several obstacles, the plan that I would transfer to another department was fulfilled within six months. Because we are in motion, the plans we focus on during these journeys become imbued with a certain momentum of their own.

Next time you take a vacation, leave yourself some loosely scheduled time to play, to think, to dream, to work magick and of course to just spend some time outdoors. You might be surprised at what you come up with and how it manifests in your life!

Ostara 2000: Reclaiming Faith

In a guided meditation this winter, one bitterly cold night in the chilly basement of a Unitarian-Universalist church, walking around an altar with a few other women, I discovered something about myself. The intent of the meditation was to discern what is of ultimate value to you, to find a thread of meaning that began in childhood and that carries through as part of your life to this day. The word that came to me was trust. Trust in the universe; trust that I would be provided for physically, mentally and spiritually. When I mentioned this to a wise friend of mine, he commented, 'I think what you really mean by that is faith.'

Faith, on the surface, seems a beautiful and hopeful word. But it hasn't always had a good connotation for me. It seemed to be 'faith, to the exclusion of logic' or 'faith, which removes your power and surrenders it to an unknown force' or 'faith, which you use to prove that you are superior because you have it.' Like religious groups who refuse medical treatment for themselves or their children because they have 'faith' their deity will heal them. Or leaving yourself awash in a blankness of days, never progressing toward your goals or even acknowledging that you have them, because your 'faith' puts action in the realm of the gods alone. Or justifying your cruelty and disdain of others by saying they are 'not of the faith,' intimating that one's own brand of faith is the only 'true' one.

To the contrary, the faith that I have begun to embrace once again is both empowering and expansive. It is the trust of a child that the universe is on your side. You feel that you are being watched over in a kindly way and, knowing that, you can work in partnership with the divine. Now I embrace and consciously nurture my faith. As I work toward my goals, on both spiritual and physical levels, I purposefully put aside doubt during the moments of challenge or difficulty, and have faith that things will work out for the best.

Having faith means trying your very best, but not in a stressful, harmful way. The 'letting go' that I feared when I was younger comes easier as I mature. Abandoning the need for control can be a very liberating experience. It means taking a break to rest when you need it, backing away from a project or situation temporarily and letting the divine work on it for you. Not giving up, but working with the natural rhythms and cycles of energy flow. It means not trying to stand in your own way, conjuring up blockages or accepting an impasse when one seems to appear, but instead cultivating faith that the solutions will present themselves just when they are needed most.

Faith is all-inclusive. My belief in the immanence of the Goddess and the God means that everyone and everything is made up of divine energy. So it makes sense to have faith in each other. By expecting people to show their best side to you, and by showing them your best side (treating them with care and respect), you will elicit a positive response more often than not.

Reclaiming my faith has brought me comfort in times of stress and trouble, and great joy when I feel in harmony with the universe. I now see the concept of faith differently: not as a crutch or excuse, but as a connection to the wellspring of life. Surrendering control to the unknown brings us more power, not less, and it is a peaceful, aware power-from-within. To me, that is indeed of ultimate value.

Ostara 2001: Magickal Stories

At this writing, though spring is hinted at in the sun's brightness, winter still has a strong hold on the land. This is the time of year when we all get a bit irritable. Most of us long for warmer weather and the ability to spend time outdoors without being so bundled up. One way to pass the time when you're snowed or iced in, *again*, is the telling of stories.

One of the members of my circle recently delighted us with a writing workshop. She gave us a series of timed writings on the theme of how magick has manifested in our lives over time. Here are three of my 'magickal stories' from that snowy evening.

My Friend Blacky

When I was almost five I wanted a cat so much. They were the most amazing, wise, magickal creatures. My Mom didn't like cats; to her they were something to be wary of or to make her sneeze. But Dad and I, animal lovers that we are, had a rare common cause. 'A cat,' he said, 'Every little girl needs a kitty cat.' And we won.

We went to pick out, from a litter of kittens born at the house of a woman I barely knew, *my cat*! I was very shy, so it was a big scary deal to go cautiously into the home of these strangers and make such an important decision. But as soon as I saw these beautiful mewing vibrant kittens, everything was okay. And there he was, staring at me without blinking, sitting up with a starched-shirt-front white spot on an otherwise mostly black body. 'Come with me, let me go with you,' he seemed to say, 'We'll have such marvelous adventures together!'

I scooped him up tenderly into my tiny hands, grinning, excited. I bundled him close to my chest, being careful not to squish him. The other kittens barely noticed his absence, though his mother must have been aware.

I named him Blacky and we developed a delightful friendship. He was my buddy for all of my imaginary adventures, the magick I created in my mind. Even Mom soon grew to like him, except when he was being feisty or ornery. He was quite a character and would put up with only a select few people touching him. He liked me, but only tolerated my little brother and stalked him as he learned to walk, knocking him face-first onto the grass.

Blacky would, as I grew older, follow us kids, at a faux-aloof distance, all through the yard, fields and woods as we played. He was my magickal pal.

The World of Books

As a teenager, the magick was in books. I wanted to escape from my failed efforts at being someone other people would like or seek out. And in a book I could go anywhere. I didn't have to talk to people and have them look at me like I was the oddest creature they'd seen all year. In books my inner sight would just open up and I'd create many pictures of all the amazing places my characters would go.

For yes, they became *my* characters, another me, part of the multi-faceted being that I was when alone. Sure, I still had my own flights of imagination. But with hormones ebbing and flowing through my body in unfamiliar waves, when I dwelt in 'real life' I had to focus on figuring out boys, why other girls were in such competition with each other and why society wanted us to buy all these things to be happy; or, more accurately, how *I* could be free to buy all of it for myself.

Books were still able to whisk me away, relax my body, excite my mind and inspire ideas and thoughts beyond the day-to-day. I ate books up like candy, brought stacks home from the library, from book fairs and yard sales. It was a safe yet thrilling way to explore the wide, diverse, mysterious aspects of the world, past, present and future.

Me, alone in my room, a book in hand, no homework left but an evening stretched out in front of me; that was magick. From book straight to dreams, filled with the characters and worlds I was reading about and with those of my own creation. I would not have said at the time that I was practicing my magick in this way, but I was. I would not have called myself a scholar, but I loved the academic part of school, even as the social aspects filled me with terror.

Remembering the Magick

I don't have a good memory in the traditional sense: remembering events as they happened, like what she said, or what color he wore. So it seems odd to me to put it this way, but I manifest my magickal aspects by *remembering*.

In the middle of a messed-up, stressed-out day, down and out, in the center of a tense room, I suddenly *remember* the magick. I take a step back, breathe a deep breath, let my laugh lines crinkle up a bit. Ah, yes, it is *all* part of magick, of God and Goddess, of creating your own material world out of the stuff, the energy, the life lessons you want to learn in that moment. I crack a sly smile at the silliness of it all.

Or perhaps I *remind* someone else, whether purposefully or by a chance comment or grin, of the same higher, broader meaning, of the prevalence of pure love throughout the universe. It doesn't matter what you call it, it's there, it's here...we are magick, magick is in us...we *are* the Goddesses and Gods and a part of the luminous All That Is.

It's hard to remember when you're in the moment, in the lesson. It's impossible to remember when your head aches and you've got to get going and the kids are fussy and the laundry isn't done, but yes, that's magickal too. It's easier to remember in those special sacred settings you create for yourself: circle meetings where the energy is crackling and people are smiling, a walk in the woods, hugs from your beloved, cats (yes, cats again) or other furry creatures rubbing up against you, swimming, dreaming.

Tell your magickal tales, enjoy the slow unfolding of the spring season, and Blessed Be!

Ostara 2002: Rain, Rain

As the traditional children's rhyme, 'rain, rain, go away, come again another day,' implies, we humans generally have a negative attitude about rainy weather. This may be even more true when spring arrives at last, the weather begins to warm up and we want to get outdoors and play. But this spring it's a little different. We're in the midst of Maine's worst drought in recorded history.

As Pagans, those who attune ourselves to the needs of the land, I suggest we change our attitudes so we can welcome and even invite the healing rain to fall. Now some of you might say, and rightfully so, that drought too is a part of the cycles of the earth. While that is certainly true, I would submit that it is more than a little likely that the activities of we humans and our consumer culture have caused the drought or at least increased its severity.

So let's look at our anti-rain culture. As we try to adjust our attitudes we can take a look at some of the symbolism of rain and, beyond soggy socks and drips in the eyes, why it makes us uncomfortable.

Rain obviously belongs to the element of water, which is often connected with emotions. Rather than seeing rain as sad or gloomy, I would suggest that it means a free flowing of emotions *through* the psyche. In this culture, we are encouraged not to cry, to cheer up and 'keep a stiff upper lip.' But as those who have given in to a storm of tears know, after crying one often feels cleansed and renewed. Letting emotions run through us is much more healthy than blocking and holding onto the energies and storing them in our bodies.

Water is also symbolic of the subconscious realms of each person and the collective unconscious we all share. The rain, as it falls through the sky (mind) onto the earth (body), can represent a more conscious awareness of the unity of all parts of life. We are not as separate as our egos would have us believe, and that can be an uncomfortable realization.

This subconscious, watery realm is also the place we visit in our dreams. Interestingly, sleeping while listening to the rain fall outside our sheltered place is one aspect of rain that many folks do enjoy. Have you noticed the quality of your sleep and dreams change when the rain falls steadily outside? And the way that it makes you want to stay in bed longer, no matter what your conscious self had planned for the day?

Water and rain are also associated with love. I admit to a fondness for rain because I fell in love one spring while taking many long walks in the rain, getting to know my new beau. We are surrounded by mainstream media that focus on either the unattainable romantic ideal or the difficulties between lovers. So perhaps it's not surprising that the happy times are associated with carefree sunny days and 'when the rain comes' is a symbol of the hard times and breakups. Contemplate instead, gasp!, a middle ground of working through emotions together, bathed in the love that makes the hard work of relationships worthwhile.

On a practical level, those of us who have gardens may be less likely to scorn the rain, even in this era of watering on demand. Similarly, our ancestors (even those of one hundred years ago) would have known the dangers of a drought. Rain is part of the cycle of life, helping to create the food that feeds us by helping plants grow, either to feed us directly or to feed the animals we use for food. While most of us get much of our food from the supermarket, this drought is a good opportunity to reconnect with the cycles of nature.

So during this spring season, whether it turns out to be particularly rainy or rather dry, give some thought to your attitude toward rain. Cry when you need to. Praise the lovely weather, even when the sky is gray and drops are beginning to fall. And if the drought does continue, consider saying a prayer to the gods, for the sake of the land and her flora and fauna, asking them to send us some healing rain.

Ostara 2004: Non-Attachment

Lately, thanks in part to my yoga teacher, I've been working with the Buddhist concept of non-attachment. At first glance, the concept might seem to be at odds with a magickal practice, but I'm finding that it helps me to be more focused and effective, and it can be quite freeing.

In order to work effective magick, we need to know what we desire. We ask 'what is our goal or aim in this endeavor?' Then we focus the intense laser beam of our will on that goal, infusing it with energy. Are we attached to the goal at that point? You bet. However, let's not forget a very important step, at the end of the spell, prayer or magical working: *letting go*. Release the energy into the cosmos and then forget about it for the time being. If we act like the little boy baking the Gingerbread Man and peek into the oven too soon, the energy we've set to work toward our goal will quickly run astray.

Non-attachment doesn't imply that we don't have passionate feelings and desires. What it does mean is that we don't get strongly attached to a specific result or outcome. As we walk our path, we can be flexible, allowing life to unfold. Of course we will put effort into those things that are meaningful to us, but we should remember that we are here to learn and grow.

A basic tenet of spellwork is to be cautious in wording the purpose of your spell. If what you really want is a car, don't do a spell for money. There are many other ways the universe could provide a vehicle for you: your brother's best friend is unexpectedly moving to Hawaii and doesn't need his Toyota, your grandmother doesn't feel safe driving anymore and wants you to have her car, or you win a new vehicle in a contest. Who knows? The point is, if you become attached to a specific outcome, a lot of opportunities that you hadn't even considered might pass you by.

Loss and change are a part of life. Non-attachment can help us to more easily adapt to them, whether we are dealing with the devastating loss of a loved one or have simply misplaced a favorite sweater.

When talking about non-attachment and relationships, don't be misled into thinking it means we must be cold, distant or withdrawn. It is more a matter of being open and compassionate with others while not letting our own expectations get in the way. We've all heard the old adage 'if you love someone, let them go.' You will get along better with others, and have more authentic relationships, if you give them the space to be themselves. You can be a more loving friend or partner when you're able to let the other person change, without clinging to your image of them.

If all of this sounds a bit much, try practicing non-attachment in one particular area of your life. Most of us have at least one mundane routine or habit, whether it's what we have for lunch, the route we drive or how we get up and get ready for the day. Even if that routine works well for you, tell yourself that you won't be attached to a particular way of doing things, just for a few days. Allow yourself to be in the moment and do what feels good or right, rather than what you 'usually' do. Notice how it feels to not be attached to a particular set of actions. You might find yourself feeling a bit more free and noticing things that you would have previously overlooked.

Oh, and as we start to move past the Equinox, one little bit of advice. Don't be too attached to warm weather. This *is* Maine, after all. Blessed Be!

Ostara 2005: Seeking Balance

As I write this, I am looking out into a cold and snowy yard, but the sunlight that pours in has a definite quality of spring. As we reach the Spring Equinox and celebrate Ostara, the days and nights are of equal length. This perfect balance of light and dark can inspire us to bring more balance into our own lives.

Spring brings us an infusion of energy as the sun's strength grows. It can be a good time to use that boost of energy to challenge ourselves, and one of those challenges can be adding things to our lives that we would not normally consider. My yoga teacher recently ran a class where we all suggested, and then did, poses that were our favorites and ones that we strongly disliked. She also suggested that we notice in our daily lives the people, things or situations that we are drawn or attracted to, and also the ones we are averse to or tend to avoid. Try it: take a few days and just observe your reactions as you go through your normal routines. It can be illuminating.

Once you have gathered some information about your own preferences and dislikes, use it to think about ways that you can incorporate more balance into your life. Some suggestions to get you thinking:

- **Adjust your social life.** If you are normally very active and social, add some quiet meditative time to your daily schedule. Or if you spend a lot of time alone, make an effort to get out more into the community and interact with others.
- **Try something new** with your magickal work. If you

participate in an active coven or circle, take some time to do some solo rituals or spellwork. If you are a solitary Pagan, attend one of the public circles or workshops being offered in your area.

- **Listen to your body.** Many of us tend to hibernate a bit in the winter, getting less physical exercise and fresh air. As the weather gradually begins to get warmer, go outside and move your body. If, on the other hand, you're a winter sports enthusiast, take a little time by the fire to relax and read a good book as the season winds down.

- **Think about the foods** you enjoy or crave and the ones you don't like, too. If you find yourself eating a lot of junk or pre-prepared food, dig out a recipe book and do some home cooking. Find some healthier alternatives that taste delicious to you as well as being good for your body. If you normally eat in a balanced and healthy way, try some new recipes or allow yourself to indulge in something decadent (can you say 'chocolate?').

- **Notice how your creativity flows** as the Wheel of the Year turns. If you've been in a receptive mode, enjoying the artistic work of others through books, movies or concerts, turn it into inspiration to pursue your own work. If you've been actively pursuing your own creativity, whether through writing, quilting or taking photos, allow yourself some stillness and time to reflect.

- **Be conscious about work.** Do you have a 'day job' that you do just to pay the bills? How balanced has your work life been lately? If you've been working a lot of hours and taking on a lot of stress, find a way to slow it down or take some time off. People in this culture tend to work a lot and get very busy, so I doubt many of us need to take on more work-for-pay. But maybe your own balance does need to shift that way. Perhaps you have a goal, such as a trip you're saving up for, and taking on more hours now would help with reaching it.

Come up with your own ideas for bringing more balance into your life at this time of the year and beyond. It can be challenging, but sometimes trying things you thought you didn't enjoy can help you to find a new talent or discover something new about yourself. Or by letting go of an activity you have long enjoyed in order to pursue something different, you may discover that as you've grown, your needs have changed in unexpected ways. Use some of that waxing sun energy to explore balance in your own way this Spring Equinox.

Ostara 2006: Tending the Spiritual Garden

Ah, spring! Although the landscape may still be a bit wintry in your backyard, the longer days and the changes peeking through as the land slowly awakens are delightful. And as the Wheel turns, we continue our steady progress toward the goals we set at Yule or Imbolc. Here at the Vernal Equinox, the days and nights are in precise balance. But we are poised on the edge of a turn towards greater solar light and energy. And though we can't yet plant our physical seedlings in the chilly ground, we can certainly take the time to tend to our spiritual gardens.

Begin by reflecting on the goals you've made for this year. If you haven't made any yet, it's certainly not too late! Once those seeds are in the ground, it's time to do the work of a gardener. Watering, fertilizing and weeding the spiritual garden, as well as making sure it's getting enough sun, will reward you with a healthy harvest later in the year.

First, the watering. Water signifies emotions. We should all know, when we're working magick, not to cling to the emotional ups and downs of a project, because we may just sabotage it. However, healthy emotions poured lovingly onto the garden will help the plants to grow. Take joy in the work you're doing toward accomplishing your goals. Share that joy and excitement with a close friend, or express it through writing or drawing in your journal or Book of Shadows. If you feel discouraged about your progress (or lack thereof) toward your goal, allow those feelings to flow through you without judging them or letting them get stuck.

You'll also want to fertilize your spiritual garden, adding important nutrients to the soil in which your projects are grounded. Make sure you have the physical-world things you need to pursue your aims. If your goal is to paint pictures, you'll need plenty of paint, good brushes, the right canvas and a work space with adequate light. If you're looking for a new home, real estate listings and transportation to potential houses will be essential. As you pursue your goal, having the support of people close to you can help nurture your spiritual garden. It can be physical support, like watching the kids or pets while you're out taking a class, or the moral support provided by encouraging words.

As the garden continues to grow, you'll want to be sure you keep it weeded. Some goals can appear daunting, but if you break them down into gradual steps, they become much more manageable. A good calendar with plenty of space to write lists is a useful tool. Be sure to take time periodically to evaluate where you are on the path to the goal. Sometimes your goal will change a bit. Or perhaps it will create lots of other exciting tangential ideas as it grows; you can 'weed' those out, writing them down to save for later. Keep your mind clear and focused by making sure your project notes and materials are organized and taking time to get out in the fresh spring air.

Be sure that your spiritual garden gets plenty of sun, so it will have the energy it needs to grow and thrive. In order to put energy into your project, or to invoke the energy of divine assistance, you'll need to be sure you are recharged. Take good care of yourself in the basic ways: eat healthy foods, get plenty of sleep and exercise regularly. In fact, doing your exercise outside will boost your spirits as well as keeping your metabolism working. Take regular breaks from your projects to pursue other activities that recharge your batteries: get a massage, have great sex, read a book, hang out with friends. Your project will still be there when you get back and you'll have more energy to devote to it.

One of the crops I'm tending this year in my own garden is my spiritual creativity. This means, in part, doing more writing. That in itself has been bringing me joy and pleasure, and I'm learning to 'let go' and not be upset when I get too busy to give it the amount of time I'd like. I'm a Virgo, so keeping my writing projects organized and well 'weeded' has been easy thus far. As long as I remember to get out and exercise regularly, I have plenty of energy to shine on my spiritual garden. And as to fertilizer, I'd like to share with you one of my new 'nutritious' venues. I've started a blog called Starcat's Study. If you get a moment to lean on your hoe and take a break from your gardening, come on by and take a look. It's at http://www.starcatscorner.com. Leave a comment if you'd like, or a link to your own web page. And may your spiritual garden flourish this spring! Blessed Be.

Ostara 2007: Spring Cleansing

As spring begins, many people deep-clean their homes, doing the traditional 'spring cleaning' to air out after winter. What about a spring cleansing for your body, mind and spirit? As we enter the lightest part of the year, we move from a balance of light and dark on the Equinox to longer days and more vibrant energies. Tap into the energy of spring, allowing its resonant music to recharge you and restore your vitality after a long and sluggish winter.

The most obvious place to start is with your body and, more specifically, your digestive system. We tend to eat more during the winter and indulge in heavier foods. If it's a safe practice for your body, try fasting, which helps clean out your digestive tract (check with a health care provider first, especially if you have any ongoing medical concerns). You can fast completely for a day, simply drinking water, or you can do a liquid fast with fruit juices and soup broth. If an entire day is too much, try a mini-fast, not eating your next meal until your body gives you clear signals of hunger, whether or not the clock tells you it's 'time for lunch.'

When you are fasting, take time to slow down and feel the sensations in your body. Notice how you feel at different times throughout the day. You may feel shaky or lighter than normal. If you feel a bit weak or dizzy, simply take some time to rest, napping or meditating. Be sure you drink plenty of water, which helps cleanse the toxins from your body. When you break your fast, begin by taking in simple foods, such as fruits, leafy greens and whole grains.

A media fast may be just the thing for a cluttered mind. We all take in many sounds and images over any given 24-hour period. Take a break, shutting off the TV and radio and saving your newspaper and e-mail for tomorrow. If anything truly important happens, you'll find out about it soon enough. Enjoy the feeling of silence, allowing the intervals between thoughts to spread out. If your mind still feels full of stray thoughts, grab a piece of paper or your journal and set a timer for 15 minutes. Begin to write whatever comes to mind, in a stream-of-consciousness manner. Don't edit or censor yourself; simply let all your thoughts flow out onto the paper. Once you are done, sit for a few moments with your eyes closed and notice how you feel.

There are many ways to cleanse your spirit. One that works well for me is to use a mantra. Pick a mantra or chant that you like, or invent one. Sit or lie comfortably with your eyes closed and focus on your breathing. Once you are completely relaxed, begin to chant your mantra, aloud or in your head. Chanting it aloud will produce a more noticeable effect, as the vibrations of the sound resonate throughout your energy system, but if you need to do it silently you will still reap the benefits. Chant the mantra over and over, letting the sounds rhythmically wash over you. Be sure you are breathing steadily as you chant. You may begin to feel the top of your head tingling. Let the vibrations of your chant resonate throughout your aura, sensing the waves of cleansing energy. When you feel ready, let the chant slowly ebb away, perhaps ending with an 'ahhh' or 'ommm' sound.

By practicing spring cleansing, you are readying your entire being for the vibrant energies of the sun's return. Once you have emptied and cleansed your body, mind and spirit, be sure to fill those empty spaces with intentional energy. Take a walk outside, absorbing the rays of the sun and the energy of the awakening earth. Find or create an affirmation that you can repeat throughout the day, bringing it to mind and focusing your energy on it. Say prayers to the earth or recite mystical poetry. Express your creativity in a way that feels joyful to you, focusing on the process and not the outcome. Take time to simply relax and enjoy the warmer weather. Happy Ostara!

Ostara 2009: Paganism in the New Age

Recently I've been studying and working with the Law of Attraction (LOA). The concept, which has been around for centuries, was recently made popular by the 2006 book and documentary *The Secret* by Rhonda Byrne. LOA is taught in more depth by Abraham, a non-physical entity channeled by Esther Hicks beginning in the 1980s. It was also explored in the Seth material, channeled by Jane Roberts, published from the 1960s through the 1980s. The basic idea of LOA is that we are each creating our own reality based on where we put our focus. The universe is made of energy and each being's perception and experience of it is unique.

Just reading the first paragraph of this article might make you squirm or want to stop reading. 'What's the difference between a

Pagan workshop and a New Age workshop? About $300,' goes a joke that's been around for a while. I often hear (or read) Pagans disparaging New Age concepts and practices and I wonder why.

As a person who is interested in consilience (the unity of knowledge, or in this case wisdom), I tend to see the commonalities among various philosophies and practices. Sure, every religion and form of shared spirituality has devotees who keep the teachings on a surface level and are most interested in being trendy. Yet it would seem that Pagans and so-called New Agers are natural allies. The Reclaiming salutation 'Co-Creators of the Multiverse' evokes images of people who are conscious of our own divinity and our participation in the unfolding of life.

What do these two distinct movements have in common? We are the ones building the new paradigm, as the old models of our civilization and culture fall away. Through conscious awareness, we are recreating the world as we work from the inside out to change ourselves and to release old patterns and blockages. We recognize that there is more to life than what we see with our five senses.

An issue some Pagans have with the New Age movement is that it focuses on self-development, perhaps to the exclusion of working toward environmental awareness and political justice. Yet what I am seeing in my contacts with others is an amazing ripple effect. As we become aware of our inner landscape, we look at our interactions with others and the earth in a new light. Even if we look through the lens of one particular issue that calls to us, such as mindful parenting, we soon find that dedication to a spiritual practice opens our consciousness in many other areas.

For example, several months ago I joined an e-mail list called 'Radical Unschooling and the Law of Attraction.' Here's a description:

Combining the philosophies of Radical Unschooling and the Law of Attraction is a progressive, revolutionary approach to parenting on the Leading Edge of Thought that we are honored to be pioneering. Radical Unschoolers choose to replace the cultural norm of using control, shame, coercion, rules and punishment with *Respect*, *Trust*, *Freedom* *Peace* and *Joy* in our lives with our children and with others.

Some of the list members are Pagan, while some are members of other religions or simply seekers wanting to do things in a new way. What we have in common is that we are all working toward parenting with consciousness. That intention, in my experience with the group and my own practice, tends to expand outward into all other facets of one's life.

Certainly, my own practice of LOA has a Pagan flavor. I include it as one of the tools I use on my path. The teachings I encounter, no matter the source, must resonate with me. This does require an ongoing commitment to self-exploration, something that most Pagans understand intuitively. We are drawn to this path because we want something more than following others' dogma. In that regard, we are individual seekers who have much in common with our New Age friends, whether they are pursuing a secular path or are already part of a religion. We are each looking for wisdom that helps us to pursue our personal goals.

There are strong similarities in some of the methods we use to create change. A simple summary of the Law of Attraction says that your thoughts and feelings determine the reality of your life. If you consciously focus them towards what you desire, it will happen. Take a look at Aleister Crowley's famous definition of magick: 'Magick is the science and art of causing change to occur in conformity with the will.'

Our will is made up of our deep desires. By getting clear about what we truly want, and then focusing on it, we create change in ourselves and thus in the world around us.

Again, an objection I've heard is that people will begin to manifest things they want, like luxury cruises and SUVs, that aren't good for the earth. This is something I've been examining as part of my journey. One answer is that since everything is made of energy, whatever we want is available to us all the time. Abraham emphasizes that there is enough abundance for every being on this planet to have all that they wish. This can be hard to grasp, particularly when we observe the natural world being mistreated by our culture's business practices.

What I've discovered is that when I look deep within myself, the things I truly wish to manifest *are* in concert with my deeply held values: building an addition to my home that enables us to heat with solar energy, traveling the world in an eco-friendly way, growing a big organic garden, writing about things that I hope will help others on their paths. As a Pagan who strives to be in touch with myself and the world on many levels, my desires dovetail with the needs and wants of the earth's spirits and beings.

Another thing that Pagan and New Age practices have in common is self-determination. If a tool or ritual doesn't work for you, there's no authority telling you that you have to use it. We employ the techniques that work best for us because we under-stand that our path is uniquely our own. Again, there certainly exist New Age gurus trying to get people to buy into their authority, but we've all heard of occasional Pagan coven leaders with questionable ethics who teach in this way. In both cases, they are the exception.

My personal study of Paganism and New Age theories (as well as Eastern philosophies) finds commonalities in the ideas of personal responsibility and power-from-within. There is no one we can 'blame' for our troubles or challenges. We are here to learn and grow, to help ourselves and others in ways that ring true for us.

As more and more people awaken to this way of living, we

encounter resistance to this expansion. You can see it in politics and mainstream religions; it is easier to follow a predetermined path and leave the tough choices up to God, the priests or the survival of the fittest. As human beings who have decided to move beyond the accepted answers and find out for ourselves how to live, I believe that Pagans and New Age practitioners have similar goals and much to learn from each other.

Chapter 5

Beltane

Beltane is a celebration of the potent fertility of the earth and all her beings. The days are longer and warmer and the world around us bursts into blossom. Our celebrations become even more festive and, as a community, Pagans gather to merrily dance the maypole and frolic on the beach. The young God, grown now to early manhood, seeks his Lady. The Goddess as Maiden revels in the flourishing of the living world around her and her thoughts turn toward finding a partner. Pagan lovers celebrate each other and enjoy the pleasures of the physical realm.

Even in northern New England, the weather has warmed enough to get outside on a regular basis and planting time has begun in earnest. Our urge is to get our bodies moving again after a winter spent mostly indoors. Fresh greens and vegetables are more easily available, in the garden or at the farmer's market. By focusing on one's body as a temple, we learn to release stress, ground more deeply and boost our self-confidence. When changes happen around or within us, we find ways to adapt and thrive. Our expansion is supported by the waxing energies of Beltane.

This blooming time of year is wonderful for reaching out. The outer world can be seen as a reflection of our inner balance of male and female energies. We might be drawn to seek a mate, improve a relationship, find new friends or volunteer in the community. Some Pagans do interfaith work, educating others about earth-based spirituality, helping to debunk stereotypes and prejudices. As we focus attention on what we love to do, our callings become clear and we can take purposeful action.

The beautiful, flowering earth is the center of attention as the fullness of spring bursts forth. We take our spiritual practices outdoors and make them part of our everyday activities. As we celebrate the qualities of the world around us, we are better able to see our own strengths. We begin to approach life and our fellow human beings with perfect love and perfect trust. We find a deeper love and respect for all life and that opens us up to further joy and creativity. Like the earth, we find ourselves in bloom.

Beltane 1997: City Witch

I just moved back to the country and found myself breathing a big sigh of relief. I was born and raised in a small Maine town and lived in rural areas until about seven years ago, when I moved to the heart of Bangor. Granted, it's not a very big city, but as a Pagan I found myself constrained in some of my activities. So here are a few words of advice on surviving and enjoying life as a city witch.

- **Mark the passage of the seasons.** This may seem obvious, but you do need to be more conscious about doing so or you'll find yourself saying 'What? It's Lammas already?' Watch the quality of the sunlight, the neighborhood cats, the foliage in your favorite park.
- **Walk wherever you can.** This gets you out into nature more often, and it can even be a benefit to city living, because you may dwell closer to your workplace, the credit union or the grocery store. Find the parks, trails along the river or shoreline, and neighborhoods with beautiful flower gardens.
- **Adapt your rituals.** This becomes especially important if you live in an apartment, where noisy chanting and dancing at midnight is not appropriate. Do quieter work, focusing more on meditation when you raise energy. Or do your rituals earlier in the day (which as a night owl doesn't

really appeal to me, but it works for some people). If you work skyclad, get thick curtains. In Maine, most people have to do rituals indoors for at least part of the year due to the extreme weather, so that aspect of city dwelling is not as much of a problem.

- **Take your vacations in the wild.** I survived so long living in town by spending my vacations, and many weekend or day trips, hiking in the woods or near the ocean. It becomes literally, as well as symbolically, a retreat from your everyday reality. You can schedule these trips around Sabbats or Esbats and perform your rituals outdoors.

- **Use the variety of resources available to you.** Some of my favorite places to go include used bookstores, the library, thrift shops and funky little cafes. Go enjoy some live music. Buy herbs in bulk at the health food store or get a deal on candles at a discount store, without having to go too far out of your way.

- **Attune yourself** to the energy of the place you live. Energy patterns run differently in the city, with many people and lots of machines. But if you are in tune with your surroundings, your own magick is more effective and can have a positive effect on those around you. As an aside here, I will mention that as a fairly open Pagan (I don't flaunt it, but I have Goddess stickers on my car and a stained glass pentacle in the front window) I have had no problems at all with prejudice from my neighbors. With some exceptions, most people in a city setting (in Maine at least) are of the 'live and let live' mindset.

These tips have worked for me during the past few years. But just the same, I do feel more relaxed now that I live out in the woods. I can have a big garden, the stars are more visible at night and I don't have to listen to cars and sirens all the time. I can do my rituals outdoors under the moon and I don't need to worry about disturbing the neighbors. Best of all, I'm in closer touch with Mother Nature.

Beltane 1998: A Radical Notion

The radical notion that I ask you to consider this Beltane season is very simple: stress is a matter of choice. You can choose not to stress out, and if you are feeling stressed, on some level you have chosen to react that way. We tend to view stress as an external factor: 'You look upset.' 'Well, I'm under a lot of stress right now.' We blame it on the stressful society we live in. However, it is really freeing to look at stress in a different way: as a deliberate, chosen reaction.

We can examine stress on a purely rational, mental level, but if we want to become aware of stress as only one option of many, we need to look at the physical body's instinctive reactions as well. That's where we hold and store tension. When something happens that we must react to, it helps to stop and see how it feels in your body. People arguing or yelling angrily, even if it is not directed at me, makes my stomach tense up. Then I begin to breathe less deeply, which is the opposite of what I need to do to remain centered in a tough situation. By bringing these subconscious reactions into conscious awareness, I can remember that I do have a choice in how I feel, react and behave.

It also helps to develop and practice healthy coping mechanisms, things that make you feel good on the physical, mental and spiritual levels. Things like exercise, sex, a soak in a hot bath, ritual, relaxing with a good book, meditation, hanging out with friends or whatever brings you joy.

Another important part of letting go of stress is to bring the spiritual realm into your everyday routine. Most of us honor the Sabbats and Esbats, but I've discovered recently that incorporating devotions and blessings into my daily life makes an amazing difference. Silver Ravenwolf emphasizes the importance and value of devotions in a Pagan spiritual practice in the first chapter of her book *To Stir a Magick Cauldron*. I've also been doing a daily three-card Tarot reading for almost a year now and seeing the patterns the cards form day after day helps me look at the bigger picture and see how what I might consider a stressful situation on a given day actually fits in with the larger cycles of my life.

We all get caught up in the mundane aspects of daily physical existence at times, which can make us as stressed-out as many of the other members of our fast-paced society. But by stopping to examine our push-button automatic reactions and realizing that we do have control over how we view reality, we can have more fun and be happier, healthier people. This tends to have a ripple effect, with other people observing your actions and attitudes and beginning to examine their own choices regarding stress.

And there's so much to do when you don't bother to be stressed! Noticing changes in the seasons, playing, dancing for no apparent reason. I know, I know – it's a radical notion! Relax and Blessed Be.

Beltane 2000: Alternative Religions' Night Out

As spring was dawning, I had the privilege of attending an excellent panel discussion on Paganism. Sponsored by the University of Southern Maine's Pagan Students Association, the discussion was part of USM's Religion and the Human Experience series. It was titled 'The Faces of New England's Non-Mainstream Religions.' The six panelists were all very knowledgeable and eloquent spokespersons for their traditions. Let me introduce them to you:

- **Andras C.A.,** a self-described Scottish witch and Pagan priest, is the director of the Earth Spirit Community in Western Massachusetts, founded in 1980 (see www.earth-spirit.com for more details). He was taught by members of a family tradition of Scottish witches.

- **Marilyn P.**, the EarthTides solitary representative, is a Quaker witch practicing the Reclaiming tradition. She described the similarities between Wicca and the Quaker religion: a belief in nonviolence and Divine immanence, taking personal responsibility, a non-hierarchical structure and a commitment to social activism.
- **Kay Gardner**, a Dianic Wiccan initiated by Z. Budapest, is a musician, ordained clergywoman and member of the Fellowship of Isis based in Ireland. She is the founder of Iseum Musicum, a three-year school for priestesses in the Bangor area.
- **Jennifer M.**, Wiccan high priestess and Christian mystic, is an ordained clergywoman and sacred tattoo artist. She follows a Christianity not informed by dogma or the church but by the teachings and life of Christ. Jennifer has an 'affinity to being a facilitator to others' spiritual experiences,' and teaches that divinity is within all of us. Creating sacred art to honor all facets of the divine is important to her practice.
- **Bill D.** is an Asatrua and member of the Raven Kindred North in Massachusetts. The Asatru worship Norse gods, and their tradition has its roots in ancient Scandinavia. It is based on seeking personal individual excellence in order to better support your community. He debunked the Viking stereotype, saying 'it's great to be a big strong guy, but it means nothing if you have no place to go home to.'
- **Sarah W.** is a Hellenistic reconstructionist, mask maker and founder of the Artists of Dionysus, an organization aimed at creating art in the service of the gods. She is also a member of Kin of the Old Gods coven in Portland. Sarah describes herself as a 'ritualist,' and explained that through direct experience with the gods, she feels a 'constant process of deepening.'

The discussion was lively and fun. While the different viewpoints of the panelists on some issues were evident, they were handled with respect. A good-sized audience, including many Pagans, posed a wide range of questions. There were some questions about particular deities and details on Pagan history, but many of the questions were more general.

Even the broad questions were addressed in what was often a personal context by the panelists, as you might expect from those who believe that one's spirituality is self-directed. Asked to define 'religion,' three of the panelists described why they prefer the term 'spirituality.' Jennifer M. discussed religion as a system of spiritual discipline, and said that although the system one uses is somewhat arbitrary, the discipline itself brings rewards.

In response to a question about the nature of faith, Kay replied: 'Faith, to me, is something you believe in even though you have no proof, and there is plenty of proof.' An audience member asked about the panelists' conception of the divine. Andras responded that to him it was 'a deep, visceral, soul-felt experience,' impossible to describe with words. He added that Paganism is the 'only religion on the planet whose original founding teachers are still present,' referring to the rocks, trees, waters, animals, wind, the earth itself.

The panelists were asked about their experience of a defining, 'epiphany moment.' Marilyn's was 'discovering, as a woman, that I too was made in the divine image.' Kay, as a musician, was inspired to discover that ancient women musicians were priestesses of the Goddess. Bill admitted he hadn't had that moment yet, which earned sympathetic laughter from the audience. He went on to describe his understanding of the Web of Wyrd, the patterns of karma in your life. He said it simultaneously brought him 'the darkest terror' and was 'most liberating' to realize that he's responsible for everything that happens in his life.

A question was raised about what types of community service the panelists were involved in. Most of them are environmentally active and also work to educate the public about what Paganism is. Marilyn discussed EarthTides and the work of helping Pagans network with each other. Others mentioned bringing art to the community, volunteering at soup kitchens and blood drives, and the importance of living a life that is ethical and socially responsible. The Pagan Student Association's mission to promote tolerance and understanding in the religious community at USM was also discussed.

The final question was: 'What are the biggest challenges now facing the neo-Pagan community?' Andras' reply was that we need to focus on creating Pagan culture and promoting and living Pagan values in a mainstream culture that is mostly Christian-oriented. Marilyn felt our challenge lies in educating the larger community about Paganism without feeling we have to present a united front. She said we shouldn't be afraid of our differences. As a Dianic Wiccan, Kay said that an important challenge is to let men know they're not excluded from the focus on the feminine divine. Jennifer spoke of ensuring that our teachers and clergy are prepared for the influx of interest in Pagan religions, and also of sustaining ourselves financially. Sarah said the challenge for the Pagan community is to make our practice part of our daily lives. Bill said the Asatru have not been considered part of 'mainstream neo-Paganism' until recently, so their challenge is 'to find our place in the Pagan community.'

This panel discussion was stimulating, entertaining and inspiring. The panelists and the questions were excellent and the debate was lively but civil. I send many thanks to the Pagan Student Association for it and look forward to more such events.

Beltane 2001: Inner Male and Female

The birds are building nests and singing cheerfully in the woods next to my new home. There are crocuses in many gardens and my Mom's daffodils are preparing their buds for blooming-time. All the hardwoods have buds too, and after a recent warm spell,

I notice that green grass has suddenly sprung up everywhere.

Even the human beings are awakening after a long winter. Everyone is talking about their new exercise programs, and when asked the routine 'How are you?' at work in the morning, people are more likely to respond 'Good,' with enthusiasm. Our inner fires are stirred to life after a long winter.

Beltane in Maine and the fertility of the Goddess and God is in evidence everywhere. It's time to celebrate their sacred union, and beyond the obvious outward signs, we can also let our inner work reflect this marriage of spirits.

We are each a blend of those various energies that we label 'male' and 'female.' It can be helpful at this time of year, and all the better if it is done while sitting outdoors on the ground, to contemplate and celebrate your unique characteristics. Whichever gender you have chosen for this lifetime, you possess inner qualities of each in varying proportions.

Consider these qualities in terms of the elements:

- **Air** relates to the mind and is considered male. How does your mind work? When you are 'lost in thought,' what types of ideas come to you? What inspires you? Do you enjoy using logic to solve problems or puzzles?
- **Fire** is passion and also corresponds to male energies. How are you active? What do you do for the protection of self and others? How would you describe your sexuality? How do you handle anger?
- **Water**, a female element, is concerned with emotion. Do you remember your dreams? What are the psychic abilities that you use most often? Who and what do you love most? When was the last time you let yourself cry freely?
- **Earth** is about physicality and is female in nature. How do you nurture yourself and others? What grounds you? Are you taking good care of your body? What do you do to take care of the earth and give back to her?

- **Spirit or ether** is that which is beyond either male or female. What activity do you consider to be the most sacred or spiritual? Do you give yourself time to meditate? What would you say is your soul's purpose?

As you consider some of these questions and make up your own, feeling free to change the correspondences to suit your needs, here are a couple of things to keep in mind. First, let the joy of Beltane permeate your being and freely celebrate all of your qualities. You are a special being, beloved of the divine. Feel the sacred union of your inner female and male energies. Second, if there are qualities that you feel you would like to explore or expand in order to be more balanced, declare your intention to allow that expansion in your life at this time. Create opportunities to act on that intention: have a good cry to get your emotions flowing or take a class in something that interests and challenges you to sharpen your mind power.

This time of year, as we turn outward once again, it is important to be mindful that the world we perceive is a reflection of who we are. You are the Goddess and the God, and the beautiful Child that they have created. You are as much a part of nature as the spring grass, the blossoms, the mother raccoon nursing her babies, the father bird protecting his nest. This season, celebrate yourself and the unique gifts you can give to the world. Enjoy!

Beltane 2002: We Are the Earth

The arrival of spring and the blossoming into Beltane, draws our attention to the fertility and magick of the earth. All of her cycles are beautiful and essential, but the contrast of moving from the harsh quiet of winter to the awakening and unfolding of spring is striking. An obvious focus on our connection to the earth is grounding.

As Pagans we often speak of all life, including ourselves, as sacred. But how many of us are truly grounded in our body on a regular basis? I hear Pagans, like other modern people, say they are stressed out and busy, lament about being overweight or complain of chronic illness or pain.

There are many ways to bring the spiritual concept of being grounded and rooted in the earth into our daily lives.

One is exercise. I'm not talking about forcing oneself to go to the gym and sweat (unless that's what you prefer). I mean moving your body, on a regular basis, in a way that brings both pleasure and release: dancing, going for a hike or a walk in the woods, riding your bike or playing volleyball with friends. Complement your active exercise with some stretching. My own practice of yoga is helping me become more aware of what it feels like to be fully present in my body, and it's a lovely feeling.

Another aspect is good nutrition. Be aware of what you put in your body and how it affects you. Again, I don't mean that we should obsess about food or count every calorie. But many of us, myself included, are ignorant or lazy about what it means to eat a balanced diet. And beyond this basic knowledge, each body is different. Learn what works best for you. I have discovered that refined sugar has a negative effect on my body and that avoiding it or eating it only sparingly makes me feel better physically and also more stable emotionally. Experiment and discover your own nutritional truths. Grow some of your own food; a very earthy, grounding process.

Rest is also important in being a grounded person. A friend recently told me about a new theory of sleep, where one would take half-hour naps five or six times a day and that would be the extent of your sleep schedule. My first thought was 'why?' In our culture, we often wish we had time to 'do more,' and we often fill up our lives with cerebral pursuits, like computer work, writing, watching TV or movies, having discussions, etc. However, like the earth, which fully rests each winter, we should respect our own cycles of mental and physical activity and repose. Sleep and meditation are very grounding and are a necessary part of a healthy reality.

It is, of course, possible to be too grounded. If we are overly rooted in the mundane world, we can be stubborn and resistant to change, thus blocking our growth. We can become more concerned about money or possessions than is healthy. Here, too, rest can help, for as our bodies sleep, we are free to dream and explore the other realms. When feeling too earthy, we can also keep in mind the plant devas, gnomes and other faeries of the earth. They don't take themselves too seriously; they play and frolic, enjoying the bounty of nature. Lighten up and take a 'play break,' doing something whimsical and fun that you wouldn't normally do.

Take some time this Beltane season to think about your relationship to the earth and your role as part of her body. Allow yourself to sink your roots deep into the soil, sending up branches which may then, with the help of the sun (passion or will) and rain (your emotions), sprout beautiful leaves, flowers or fruit. Enjoy the pleasurable feelings of your body, of just being without having to strive or worry. Ground yourself in the Mother. Blessed Be!

Beltane 2003: Perfect Love and Perfect Trust

One of the tenets of some Pagan paths, often heard at Beltane in particular, is 'in perfect love and perfect trust.' Just what does this mean? Beyond the bounds of our coven, how can we welcome this idea into our lives?

It's scary to trust, because many of us were raised not to trust anyone fully, not even ourselves. We question our intuition until it no longer comes knocking. We're told not to talk to strangers, don't leave your valuables unattended, make sure you double-check your bank statement. Don't listen to your body to find out when you're hungry, but eat at noon and 6pm regardless.

In the area of romance, it gets even more sticky. The concept of having 'the one perfect mate' is something I question, but that's a whole other essay (or book). But even given that notion, you're supposed to subtly (or, for the more paranoid, covertly) check up on your boy- or girl-friend to make sure they're not 'cheating' on you. You may gossip about your mate's short-comings behind their back. It is almost expected that there'll be some dishonesty involved in romantic relationships.

What if there wasn't? What if you and your loved one(s) agreed that perfect love and perfect trust would be what you'd aim for? First of all, what does 'perfect' mean? It means that there's no failing. Love gives you another chance and so does trust. But does it? You have to overcome a lot of programming to be able to give someone another chance once they've lied to you. To deal with them without suspicion from that point on is challenging, to say the least. And there can be a fine line between forgiving others and being a doormat, if they continue to regularly exploit your trust.

But say you do trust and love each other, as near to perfectly as possible. How liberating! You grow to trust yourself, and furthermore, to trust in the universe! You realize that all the energy you once spent lurking around (whether literally or in your head), waiting for someone to screw up, is now available for other things. The time you spent worrying about not getting what you need in life is now yours to spend in joyous ways.

I think perfect love and perfect trust, once you invest in them, begin to ripple outward, affecting your entire life and that of those around you. Instead of assuming that strangers or acquaintances are 'out to get you' in some way, you can be more open and real with them. That type of open and positive energy will resonate with people subconsciously and they are then more likely to return it in kind.

Living this way doesn't mean being stupid, like leaving wads of cash on your car dashboard, but it does mean trusting that you, in league with the universe, can take care of yourself and that there is more than enough love for all of us.

Beltane 2005: Beyond Self-Doubt

So, how's your self-image? No, really. If you answered (honestly) 'good' or 'great,' you can turn the page now and get on with celebrating Beltane. But if you're less than satisfied with the way you feel about yourself, read on. We've all heard the clichés about how many of us, especially women, suffer from a poor self-image, living as we do in this culture filled with media images of conventionally beautiful, happy, rich people leading exciting and successful lives. But hey, we're Pagans, we live alternative lifestyles where diverse attitudes, paths and body types are equally valued. Right?

Even in the Pagan community, where acceptance of diversity is most often the norm, it seems that the very people who welcome others without question are still quite, well, hard on themselves. A man known in the community for his intelligence and big-hearted inclusiveness of all points of view berates himself for that very asset, saying he's too 'wimpy' or 'wishy-washy.' A kind and sensitive woman whose insight encompasses many worlds feels like she's being 'too much of a downer' when she shares the depths of her difficult inner work in circle. And many of us, myself included, lament our physical appearance and its deficiencies.

Let's focus on body image as an illustration. Much of the time, I feel pretty good about myself. But from time to time, especially just after a long winter, I catch a glimpse of my body in a mirror and there it is: my 'weight problem.' My immediate thought is 'that's not the way it feels like I look!' But why not? Shouldn't my self-image be more in line with what I really look like? When I gain a few extra pounds, shouldn't I be able to integrate them into my being? Or should I, over time, be able to create a physical self that is reflective of my inner feelings and self-perception? And why do I use food as a comfort in times of stress, rather than relying on my understanding of good nutrition?

After wrestling with these questions and self-doubts off and on over many years, here's a fairly recent insight. If I change my focus and concentrate on my spiritual growth and lessons, on walking my soul's path, then over time my outer shell will come to reflect this essence. If the goal is spiritual health, then one's appearance and behavior will follow the soul's lead. Cosmetic changes, whether to the body or the personality, cannot be the primary goal or the changes will be superficial, imposed upon the self rather than arising naturally from within. Focus on the things that are truly important, in the long-term sense, and true beauty cannot but follow.

When you find yourself in doubt of your appearance or abilities and wanting to create change, it is important to be gentle. Treat yourself as you would a beloved child or friend. Ask yourself where the impulse is coming from. Reassure yourself of your good qualities or ask a loved one to remind you. Sit in silence and let your thoughts flow by, listening without judgment. Find your inner voice, your intuition and ask it what positive action you can take. It may surprise you to find the suggestion has more to do with changing your attitude than with adjusting your lifestyle.

When you experience feelings of self-doubt or shame, stop for a moment and take a deep breath. Practice a simple grounding exercise. Sometimes these feelings point to a need for self-nurture. You may feel fat because you haven't taken a walk in the fresh spring air this week, or feel stupid because you're overtired and you need to give your weary brain and body a good night's sleep. Or maybe you've been focused too much on your work or on caring for others and what you're seeking is some time to turn inward.

As Pagans, we're used to being respectful of others and the uniqueness each person brings to this earth. We are also accustomed to 'working on ourselves.' But as human beings and members of a particular culture, we are still susceptible to feelings of inadequacy and self-doubt. What we have, and can use, are the tools to dive beneath the surface, to find our true self-worth and follow our own path, even if it is a 'road less traveled.' And that's worth celebrating.

Beltane 2006: Tending the Temple

I've noticed over the past few years, among the Maine Pagan community, the reflection of a trend that's happening throughout the US. Many of us are overweight and not taking good care of our bodies. It would seem that Pagans, closely tied as we are to the natural rhythms of the earth and nature, would more carefully listen to the needs of our physical bodies as well as those of the spirit. However, 'all acts of love and pleasure are Her rituals,' and indulging in comfort food or snuggling on the couch reading rather than exercising, can certainly bring pleasure.

This column isn't intended to make you feel guilty, so that you start a crash diet or rush out and buy an expensive gym membership. On the contrary, taking good care of one's physical 'temple' is about balance and can be full of pleasure and joy. And at this time of year, when the weather is fair and spring is blossoming, it's easy to get outside for exercise and fun. Here are some tips to get you started or to add some variety to your own routines:

- **Home cooking** tastes better. As well as being better for us, with less added sodium, fat and preservatives, a good home-cooked meal truly tastes better. You can add in love and positive energy as you stir and chop. No time to cook? There are lots of recipes that are 'quick and easy' while still using fresh and healthy ingredients. Get a cookbook from the library or search for recipes on the Internet. Cook meals ahead on your day off and freeze them in appropriate portions to use throughout the week.

- **Try sensible weight loss.** Restrictive diets don't usually work; they make us feel resentful and deprived and can lead to binge eating. If you need to lose weight, do it in a slow and sensible way. A simple, free and sustainable way to eat is the 'No S diet.' It's as easy as this: no seconds, no snacks and no sweets, except on days beginning with the letter 'S.' You choose what and when you eat, but stick to three basic meals (or more frequent but smaller ones, if that works better for you). On weekends, you can indulge. It's a great way to gradually and sensibly lose weight. For more information you can visit the website of the guy who created it, http://nosdiet.com.
- **Exercise** makes you feel better. I'm not just talking about physical health; regular exercise also helps you feel more calm and centered on an emotional level. It relieves emotional stress and helps you view your life with equanimity. When we're more centered, we can better deal with life's ups and downs and be in a better space to help others.
- **Refined sugar and caffeine add stress.** These types of foods are fine in moderation, but relying on them to get through each day puts a serious strain on your body and emotions. If you require caffeine to get going in the morning, or rely on a 'sugar high' to get you through an afternoon slump, think about how you can modify your reliance on these addictive substances. Once you're able to even out your blood sugar a bit, then those foods and drinks can become 'special treats' enjoyed as part of your balanced diet, rather than 'must haves' that add unneeded calories and strain the body's systems.
- **Walking** is the best-kept fitness secret. Rather than working out in a smelly indoor gym or pushing yourself to jog when your joints groan at the thought, simply take a walk. It gets you outside, in nature, which in itself lifts the

spirits. And it provides high-quality exercise with very little strain. If time is a concern, make your daily walk serve more than one purpose. You can turn it into a moving meditation, use your walk to observe the seasonal changes of the land where you live, mentally plan your day as you go or walk with a friend and socialize along the way.

- **Household chores** burn calories. Working in the yard and garden, vacuuming and mopping, hanging out clothes: all these things can be part of one's exercise routine, especially if you approach them with enthusiasm and energy. Put on some upbeat music and clean the living room. You have to do these things anyway, so dance around as you go, making it fun and getting your body moving.

- **Skip the TV.** Watching TV is not only a passive activity, it also leads us to snack on the junk foods we see advertised there. I know several families, my own included, who don't own a television and aren't missing anything. Yes, everyone needs 'down time' to relax, but you can read a book or magazine, or play a game. And when you're done, you naturally move on to the next thing you feel like doing, such as taking a walk or doing some yoga, without getting 'sucked in' to endless remote clicking.

- **Get plenty of sleep.** It's good for your body, but also for your spirit. If you're getting plenty of sleep (most adults need seven or eight hours each night), you're also allowing yourself plenty of time for dreaming. You'll remember your dreams and can work with them as part of your spiritual practice. And sleep also helps us be emotionally grounded and mentally alert, a good combination for ritual work as well as life in general.

- **Try some spiritual exercise**. My favorite is yoga, but there's also tai chi or the various types of martial arts. The idea is to exercise the body while also working with your energy system and spiritual principles. A regular practice helps you get outside of the flow of time, bringing you between the worlds and helping you to see your life in a 'big picture' way. Start slowly. There are affordable classes available in many towns as part of the school system's 'adult ed' offerings. Or you can get a CD or tape which leads you through a simple routine. You don't have to commit to doing it every day to reap the benefits.

These are just a few suggestions for improving and maintaining your physical health. Take what you will and leave the rest. Find your own balance and create your own practices for healthy living. You'll find that it not only 'keeps the doctor away,' but also contributes to the depth of your rituals and spiritual work. Blessed Beltane to you!

Beltane 2007: Joyful Intentions

When doing magick, the key to successful spells is to have a clear intent, which you can then empower with energy. The same is true of life as a whole. Your entire life is a magickal act. Everything you do is sacred. So it is important to empower your life and everything you do in a way that supports your spiritual journey. How can you do this on a day-to-day basis? Consider it an ongoing ritual – every place is sacred, each person, animal or object is divine and the way you use your energy creates the situations you encounter (think of the Threefold Law).

To find your true intentions, really listen to yourself. You might say your greatest joy is eating jelly doughnuts – but go deeper. Peel away another layer of what you've been taught by your family or absorbed from the media, the culture, the advertisements all around us. Take yourself back to when you were a small child. What kind of things did you most enjoy doing? Drawing? Making up songs? Playing ball? Think about how you've developed these talents or inclinations throughout your lifetime. Doubts or fears might arise ('how can I make a living as a songwriter?') but let those fade away and focus on the feelings you get when you're doing what you love to do.

Now think about all the things that inspire you to be creative. What makes your creative energy flow? A dream you had? A beloved person? A beautiful scene in nature? Richly colored fabric? See yourself in your mind's eye, inspired by your own personal muse. What would you create? How would you express the excitement and energy flowing through you at that point? Those are the things you came here to do!

So, now, your fun and exciting 'job' is to manifest those things in your life. You can do this in a natural and joyful way, even if your current lifestyle is different from what you envision. Whatever you're doing, you can be yourself and bring your creativity to it. Creativity isn't just about art or writing or music, it's in how you live your life. It's about putting your full intention and attention on what you're doing. When you're in tune with who and where you are, you're in tune with the universe and you can see that everything you need is there, being presented to you as a beautiful gift.

Whatever you want more of in your life, be that. As the saying goes, 'act as if.' Be the way you want your world to be. As you change yourself, the universe will flow in the direction you choose. If you want to be a writer, write three pages in your journal every day. Start a dream journal and write in that every morning, then use those ideas to inspire further creations. If you want to write a novel, start now and write for just 15 minutes every day. You can find 15 minutes to practice what you most enjoy, even in a full and busy life.

You may have been taught that walking your spiritual path is hard 'work,' but really it's about relaxing into your life, becoming your true self in the most comfortable and natural way. Find what you most love to do, what brings you great joy and then – do that more! Find the people who encourage your self-expression and creativity and fun – and be with them! You are here to express the unique self that you have created on this plane and that is the most exciting and fun thing you can do. Of course there will be challenges and obstacles along the way. They are there to help you learn and grow even more, to hone your courage and determination, to make you even more creative in how you live your life. By living your joyful intentions, you'll find yourself achieving the things you've dreamed of, in harmony with your soul's purpose, and enjoying every moment. What could be more fun than that?

Beltane 2008: Navigating the Seas of Change

As I write this, I'm in a phase of intense transition. I have 22 days left (and counting) at my longtime day job and then I'll be pursuing my dream of writing for a living and homeschooling the kids. I created this change, I'm excited about it and it feels like the right choice and good timing. Yet even so, I'm feeling the stress of breaking out of a comfortable routine and into the unknown. This time of transition, when I'm not really in my old world and haven't yet arrived in the new life either, is a strain. Whether or not we've asked for change, it can certainly mess with our equilibrium. It feels like navigating through uncharted and sometimes stormy waters.

When you're on a ship out on the open ocean, it will constantly be in motion. You have to get used to the surfaces under your feet and their rolling rhythm, or you won't be able to move around, and you might even get seasick. When your life is in a state of change, there is often a lot going on and things happen in an unfamiliar rhythm. Your normal routine is interrupted. If you can find your balance in that space, becoming centered within the motion, you'll be better able to function. Becoming adapted to the changes going on around you helps you choose the direction you wish to sail.

Seeing the big picture can also be useful. Look through your spyglass and see what's out there on the horizon. If the change you're negotiating is a planned one, remember the goals and timelines you've set for yourself. In less than a month, I'll be working at home and choosing the structure of my days. When I'm frantically trying to fit in meetings and reports on the time schedule of my current employer, it helps to remember this. If your state of change was unplanned, such as an illness, accident or unexpected change in a relationship or residence, it can help to envision what you want your life to be like in a month, six months or a year. Populate your horizon with tropical islands, exotic ports or a glimpse of home shores.

Taking breaks to spend time in nature always helps. Even as Pagans, we sometimes forget to stop toiling and come up on the deck to look around. On the ocean, the constantly changing skies remind us of the transience of our own weather system (our moods and states of being). Getting outside to observe the changes in seasons refreshes us and infuses us with the energy of the divine. Just as the snow finally melted, we'll see that our challenges and changes will eventually pass. Go outdoors.

Sometimes you just need to find a place to drop anchor for a bit. In the midst of the seas of change, find something that gives you a quick, healthy break, leaving you feeling renewed. Your anchor will reflect your personal needs and interests. My daily three-card Tarot reading, which I've been doing for more than ten years now, gives me a centered place from which to start the day. You might take a brisk ten-minute walk, play a video game or put on your favorite song and dance around wildly. Be careful not to anchor yourself to something that could become an unhealthy habit and ultimately add to the chaos, like caffeine or other drugs. I have to watch my sugar intake when I'm stressed out; if I eat too much of it, my emotions get out of control, increasing my stress rather than alleviating it. Getting plenty of sleep is also key. Your body needs rest and your soul needs time to dream, which is especially important when you're actively creating a new way of being.

Change is a fact of life. It will come and find you even if you don't actively seek it out – and why wouldn't you? Exploring new horizons is fun! Our life's voyage will have plenty of uncertainty, but there are ways to sail the seas with grace and joy. Take good care of yourself and you'll learn to enjoy the trip, even without a detailed map.

Chapter 6

Litha

Ah, summer! Litha, the Summer Solstice, is the peak of the sun's power, a time of long, warm days. The crops have all been planted and the main harvest festivals are yet to come. It's our chance to take a break from our normal routines, perhaps taking a vacation or simply spending more time outdoors. On Midsummer Eve, the Goddess and the God spend time enjoying each other's companionship. It's also a favorite time for the faeries and elemental nature spirits to frolic, and we can take a cue from them about allowing ourselves more leisure and playfulness.

During the more relaxed days of Litha, we take a step back and look at the bigger picture of our lives. We celebrate the progress we've made towards our goals and marshal our energies for the work still in front of us. There is time to examine how we make a living in this world. We look more closely at our work and our callings, seeing how ongoing challenges help us to grow. The lazy days of summer provide an opportunity to celebrate both work and leisure. In the stretch of days between planting and harvest, we tend our spiritual gardens with attentive weeding and watering.

As the Sun God enjoys the height of his power, we too can feed our inner and outer fires. Summer is the perfect time for fine-tuning how we live in our bodies, how we use our energy. As we pause to rest, the world of the senses opens up and we can release pent-up stress. Strenuous exercise feels good, as does swimming and sunbathing. We open to exploring silence, learn to let go of persistent worries and fears and make peace with grief and other deeply-held feelings. As we soak up the long, warm summer days, we recharge ourselves for the coming work that the harvest-time will soon bring.

Litha 1997: Mazzim

This column may seem different than the other, essay-type ones I've written. But I'm upset and I feel a strong need to write about it (and in fact I feel like I'd be dishonest if I didn't). My feline friend and familiar (although that word means different things to different Pagans), 'Zim, disappeared on the last day of May.

She is three years old, but small and slim, with an Abyssinian build and a tiger-striped multi-colored (mostly brown and black) coat, white paws and chest. She's very joyful and loving, yet wary of strangers. She has been an indoor cat most of her life, but since we moved to a more rural area a few months ago she has enjoyed exploring the outdoor world. But given her personality, I wouldn't have expected her to just wander off.

The most difficult part is not knowing where she is or what happened to her. I would expect that this would be the best time to use magick: when I really need it. Yet my ability to be objective is gone, so it seems like my power-from-within has deserted me, too. It's the 'healer, heal thyself' conundrum: I'm just too close to the situation. If my intuition says she is still alive and well, then I think I'm just being optimistic; if I feel that she has died, I feel like I'm getting paranoid.

I have outlived several animal companions in my life, as well as several humans. Those times, although I was sad and grief-stricken, my faith in the gods and the natural order helped me through. I got past the grief and have good memories of, and even contact with, those who died. But this situation is different in two ways: one, I don't know for sure if she is alive or dead. I'd rather know than imagine she is suffering, perhaps hurt or hungry somewhere. My hopes that I'll see her when I get up in the morning or at her dinnertime in the evening, keep rising and then falling again. The second difference is that she is so young. Most of the others I know who have died have been further along in their lives – maybe not elderly, but at least middle-aged! I see no reason why she would be taken away so young.

Perhaps the key word there is 'see;' although I can't understand the reasons for this tragedy, they do exist. Yet because I can't 'see' or 'touch' them, I begin to doubt. I question the wisdom of the God and Goddess and that makes me feel worse, not better. I question the usefulness and validity of my own power, to seemingly 'abandon' me when I need it (what good is a fair weather witch?!). With every day that goes by I miss her a bit more. Cats have been my favorite totem since I was a baby (hence my magickal name), so I wonder what I've done to earn their displeasure; what message is being conveyed here?

This all sounds very despondent and although those feelings are real, others are present too. I am thankful for the gift of the time she did spend with us and the love she gave. I have hope that she is happy wherever she is and even that we'll see her again. I know that 'Zim need answer only to herself and her feline gods; she makes her own choices. I have good friends who freely give of their energy and magick to help both 'Zim and I. And I still do my own rituals for her and visit her in my dreams.

Litha 1998: Making a Living

Wow, I can hardly believe its Midsummer already! Lately I've been thinking about employment and how it fits in with a Pagan lifestyle. In this culture, our personal worth is often judged by what we 'do' for work. 'What do you do?' is a frequently heard question when meeting someone new. It is implied in the question that your answer won't be something like: 'Well, I do a lot of hiking and I read quite a bit.' They want to know about your career, profession or job.

I've been struggling lately with the concept 'do what you love and the money will follow.' I am certain that it works, but the timeframe is often different than we might wish. Getting your own business off the ground, if that's what you'd love to do, takes time and usually a financial investment. Some of the things we'd love to do require a degree or further study and that can cost quite a bit in both money and time. Some fields are difficult to break into, such as writing books for a living. Meanwhile, we may feel stuck in a job that is not really what we want to do or find ourselves looking for work that will help us 'get by.'

In the meantime, even if you live a fairly simple life, there are always expenses involved. Everyone needs to buy food and clothing (though it is cheaper if you grow and make your own), to pay for a place to live and usually to cover the cost of transportation (and if you have your own vehicle, insurance and registration are required). There are expenses involved with health care, whether alternative, mainstream or some combination. If you are responsible for children it gets more expensive; even public education and home-schooling have their costs. Most of us have the luxury (considered a necessity in modern life) of a telephone and many folks have computers with on-line access. Add to that the occasional luxury items you may enjoy (books, a movie, a night out dancing or even bagels and coffee) and you have a pretty hefty monthly budget.

Here are some questions to get you thinking about your own way of making a living. What do you do 'for a living?' Do you work for others or for yourself? Is this your 'True Work' or do you do it just to pay the bills? If you could do whatever you wanted in terms of a job or career, what would it be? How do you reconcile the need for money, which we use in our culture to fulfill our material needs, with the desire to do only what you feel is your true work in this lifetime? Are you open about your Paganism at work? Do you feel your current job is compatible with your belief system?

Litha 2000: Letting Go
I recently heard Midsummer described as a time for 'letting go.' Now that the crops were all in, our ancestors had to let the earth

and sun work their magick and trust that the harvest would be enough to sustain them through the next turn of the Wheel. The hard work of planting was done, with the hard work of harvest still in the future, so the letting go was also a pleasant relief of burdens, a chance to be just a little bit lazy.

In our modern era, summer is a time when many of us take vacations or get outside more than usual to enjoy the warmer weather. The longer evenings stretch out in front of us, with extra time for rest and recreation. Yet I think many of us would do well to take the lesson of relinquishing control more to heart.

We no longer have to worry about the crops and whether we will have enough food, at least here in the United States. The grocery stores will stay full, one way or another. Most of us are given great control over our physical survival and have what would be considered in other times or other parts of the world to be great wealth.

Yet we do worry. We fret over money – whether we will have enough, not only for the cornucopia of food in our supermarkets, but to pay our bills and enjoy luxury items. We worry about whether we will have enough time each week to do the things we 'have to' do. And, understandably, we worry about the environment, about the state of affairs in this nation and around the world, about changing our misguided culture of power-over.

I suggest we each take time this Midsummer to let go, to give up the control we expect to have over our lives. I'm not saying we shouldn't work for change or even work towards taking that vacation we've been saving up for. But do your very best, in mundane and magickal terms and then trust that your efforts will bear fruit.

Give up a few of the things you feel you 'must' do each day or week to stay in control of your world. Chances are no one will notice or complain. Your kids would probably rather spend leisure time with you than have every last scrap of laundry done. Errands can be combined or put off until a later date (think of how much time most Americans spend buying things). Don't work so much; take time off if at all possible. Don't necessarily use this free time to rush around doing activities that are supposed to be fun, but just relax in the sun and read, take a swim or chat with a friend.

I may be 'preaching to the choir,' as the saying goes. We are Pagans and as such are more in tune with the cycles of the earth than most modern people. Yet I have noticed recently that even among my Pagan friends, there is a drive to do more and at the same time a dissatisfaction with having a busy lifestyle. Remember that you choose to work, take an evening class, give Tarot readings, bake bread for your family and try to fit in a coven meeting. Slow it down a little and see how you feel.

Take some time this season to consciously 'let go' of the results you expect from your work and your play. Let your senses be alive and delight in the joy of the warm Midsummer breezes. Blessed Be!

Litha 2001: Silence

My study of magick has included the adage 'to know, to will, to dare, to be silent.' Being silent is a key part of one's spiritual practice. Not only is it important, as implied in the above quote, to enhance the power of one's magickal workings by not talking about them. It is also necessary to allow time for some silence in our busy lives.

In our culture as a whole, silence is seen as a negative thing. Giving someone the 'silent treatment' implies coldness and anger. Silence is often interpreted as loneliness. Many people fill the silence of their lives with TV, recorded music and constant chatter. But silence can be a wonderfully expansive and joyous experience.

There are many forms of silent meditation we can use to open to our inner silence. Try traditional Eastern seated meditation; even ten or twenty minutes each day can bring amazing insights and clarity. There are many good books available to help you learn. If seated meditation doesn't appeal to you, take a silent walk, opening your attention fully to the sounds, sights and smells of the world around you. Even the simple practice of moving about your chores or tasks at home with no 'background sounds' can be refreshing.

Silence in the company of other people can be a way to open to others' energy patterns and nonverbal messages. At this moment, Quester and I enjoy a companionable silence while he reads a book and I work on this article. There is delight in simple proximity to each other. Including time for silence in circle with your coven can be very powerful. In my circle we like to use a silent hand-to-hand circle casting, and for me at least, the fact that I don't have to speak or to focus on someone else's words enhances the experience of the group's energy. If you become interested in exploring the depths of silence, try creating and performing a silent ritual. See how your group interactions change, and how they remain the same, when you are not speaking aloud.

While it may not be the most exciting-sounding aspect of the Pagan path, opening to silence can be a rewarding and deepening experience. Why not begin to explore the silence or add more of it to your regular spiritual practice?

Litha 2002: Light My Fire

As I write this article, I'm lying on a blanket in my sunny, breezy backyard. We've arrived at the height of summer and the Sun God is at His fiery best. We can see the element of fire all around us: in the sun and the green plants and colorful flowers that the warmth of its rays has nurtured.

In this culture we often idolize the youthful energy of the fire within us, yet we don't always stop to appreciate the gifts of creativity it brings or the care we should take to channel it properly. If we allow our inner fire to run unchecked, we can become 'burned out' or overly stressed, thus becoming run down and, eventually, ill. If our fires burn too low, we can feel like it is difficult to muster the energy just to get through our daily tasks.

Besides the importance of rest and 'down time' (remember those lazy days of summer?), it is also key to keep your energy system clear. It's like keeping your engine clean so the fuel can burn more efficiently – if the fiery energy that runs through you encounters a lot of blockage, it will take extra effort just to keep it running. There are many ways to 'keep clear,' and you can combine them in whatever way works best for you. Here is just a sampling: meditation, martial arts, yoga, chiropractic care, polarity therapy, Reiki, cardiovascular exercise, prayer, good sex and dancing. In addition, it's a good idea to express your creativity regularly, in whatever way you choose. That will help keep your own inner hearth fire burning.

At Midsummer, everything is in full bloom, ourselves included. Creative ideas may come to us faster than we can handle, and the energy to work on them may be present in abundance or may burn brightly at times and then unexpectedly die down to a bed of glowing embers. Allow yourself to be creative as the passion strikes you, but at this time don't try to organize or discipline yourself too much. Let yourself play and enjoy the process, rather than looking to the end results. At Midsummer we are still in the growing season, not yet having reached the time of full harvest.

Sexual passion and sensuality are also brought forth by our inner fire. Allow yourself to express that passion in ways that make you feel good. Again, be playful and lighthearted, bringing pleasure to your lovers and to yourself. Outdoor sex can be great fun at this time of year and skinny-dipping is a wonderful treat. Even if you choose not to be sexually active, take time to delight in the sensual pleasures of the physical body; try a visit to a licensed massage therapist or cook yourself a gourmet meal.

Sometimes the intensity of fire can be overwhelming or even

frightening. Where there is fear, there is power, and you can take advantage of the fact that another attribute of this element is protection. Call on your warrior spirit and channel those fiery energies into a protective force field. Just as we use sunscreen to protect us from the full effect of the sun's rays, we can set up filters that help us process the energies that we encounter daily. Filters can also help keep you from picking up unwanted energy from other people, thus helping keep your own energy system clear.

This summer, as you get out into the sunshine and enjoy the warm, long days, remember to stoke your internal fires and keep them burning brightly. Play with your energy and enjoy the pleasures of creativity and physical incarnation. Remember that you are an eternal being of light and a child of the Sun God. Brightest blessings this Midsummer!

Litha 2003: It Really *Is* a Temple

I was talking with my kids the other day about what is 'real' versus what isn't. Their concept of 'real' meant 'living.' A plastic toy horse isn't real, but the horses we see grazing in the field are. I asked the four-year-old, 'how do you know *you're* real?' First I got the 'Mom, what a silly question!' look, but when I insisted on an answer, she simply got up and started moving her body around the room. The six-year-old had more practical answers, like breathing and having a heartbeat, but I think that feeling the sensations of the body as it moves is an important piece of wisdom about our existence.

We experience the world through our body and its senses. I include here not only the traditional five senses, but also 'extrasensory' perception, which is often experienced as or accompanied by physical sensations. Did you ever 'get that feeling in the pit of your stomach' which you know is intuition, or sense moving energy as a tingling feeling or lights on the edges of your peripheral vision? One's body is the lens through which the soul experiences this world.

As Pagans, we value nature and seek to honor and commune with the natural world. But sometimes we tend to forget that we, too, are a part of nature. We may ignore the needs and desires of our bodies, working a few extra hours when we'd rather rest or forcing ourselves to sit in front of the computer to finish a project when we clearly need to stretch. Or we may indulge in behavior that feels good in the moment, but which can cause illness when done too often, like eating too many rich foods or drinking too much alcohol. Listening carefully to your body, living in it from moment to moment and following its cues, is an art that many of us forget once we move past early childhood.

Many modern Pagans, myself included, have focused on emotional, mental and spiritual growth, sometimes to the exclusion of physical well-being. As I've been learning recently, they are all really part of the same system and neglect in one area will restrict our efforts to reach new heights in the others. Also, enhancement of physical health can help with other areas. I'm finding that daily exercise helps me more easily regulate emotions such as anger and frustration (I can hear some of you thinking 'well, duh!' but hey, I've been a non-athletic bookworm most of my life).

'The body is your temple' goes the old saying. I believe that's true, but rather than being so cautious about what you ingest or encounter that all the flavor of life leaches away, I encourage you to let yourself fully enjoy some simple, healthy, pleasurable sensations. Summer is a great time to explore physical wellness. Feel your muscles move and stretch as you hike a mountain, dance to your favorite music or walk along the beach. Enjoy the flavors of fresh berries, or a salad made with veggies from your garden or the local farmers' market. Be fully present, not thinking about other things, when you kiss your lover goodnight or look into the eyes of a dear friend. Feel the sun on your skin, experience the water as you slide into the lake, breathe in the scents as you work in your garden. There's no need to be an ascetic when there are so many luscious feelings that don't have artificial flavoring.

Each body has different needs and preferences and those will change as time goes by. Experiment with new foods and different ways of moving, of sleeping, of meditating. Be honest with yourself. Maybe you *do* get pleasure from eating ice cream after every meal, but allow yourself to notice the 'crash' that comes after the sugar buzz, as well as the pleasurable sensations of sweetness and cold.

The key is to find a balance that works for you. What makes you feel 'real,' and allows you to live a healthy life? We all have health concerns; they are part of the lessons we're here to learn. But we are also perceptive enough, if we truly pay attention, to know which behaviors contribute to health and which don't. Listen and your body will tell you.

Litha 2005: Pagan Summer Fun

This Litha, let's forgo the usual serious column on how to improve your spiritual life. This one is just for fun; any character improvement that results is simply a side benefit.

A lot of folks I've talked to recently have said they had a particularly rough winter. The rather rainy spring, while feeding the trees, may not have helped lift our spirits much. But here we are, at the height of the sun's intensity, the season of the God at the peak of his masculine power. The days are long and it's time to get out and enjoy them. Some tips from your friendly feline pleasure-seeker:

- **Go barefoot** as much as possible. Go skyclad, if you're so inclined (but don't forget the all-natural bug repellent).
- **Swim** in the ocean, lake or river. Even if the water is too cold.
- **Attend an outdoor festival.** It doesn't have to be specifi-

cally Pagan; my family has fun at the Scottish Highland Games every summer, camping out and partying in the spirit of our ancestors.

- **Have a Litha Costume Ball.** Decorate your backyard with strings of lights and candles. Ask guests to dress up as faeries. Sip elaborate drinks and eat tiny sandwiches.
- **Play hooky** from your job and do nothing all day.
- **Take a midnight moon-and-stars hike.** Put red cellophane over a flashlight and look for owls (that way the light won't disturb them).
- **Curl up and read** a novel or a book of poetry in the sun.
- **Treat yourself** to a massage or pedicure. No, really! Barter for it with a friend if that sounds too expensive.
- **Hold a musical jam session.** Dance to tunes your improvised group makes up on the spot. Be sure to invite lots of drummers.
- **See a summer movie**, perhaps one with a Pagan-friendly theme, like Star Wars or Hitchhiker's Guide to the Galaxy.
- **Get a group of friends together to play** softball or kickball. Even if you're terrible at it, be goofy and have a good time.
- **Go on a fancy picnic.** Spread out an old tablecloth, break out the cloth napkins, wine glasses you got from a yard sale and candles in fancy holders. Eat and drink in style on the beach or at a music festival.
- **Climb a tree.** How long has it been?!

Have fun!

Litha 2006: Faeries, Flowers and Fun

Happy Litha! How does your spiritual garden grow? The energy of the sun is at its highest now and the fruits of summer are beginning to show. But there's still a lot of work to be done before the final harvests. Lots of weeding, watering and, yes...waiting.

You may find that you'd like some help with the work you set out to do on this time around the Wheel. Midsummer Eve is the perfect time to ask for that help from the faerie realm. It's also a fortuitous time to reaffirm your goals and celebrate the progress you've made thus far.

Faerie energy can bring a big boost to the projects you're working on. Of course, you should approach your request for help with lots of reverence and mirth. Gifts are essential: put out libations of milk or mead, and maybe add some chocolate, herbs and shiny trinkets. Leave the offerings in the forest or a flowery place in your yard. Dusk and dawn are special times for the faeries, so you may want to do some outdoor meditation, communing with them at those times when the tides of energy are turning.

If the faerie folk agree to help you, be sure you're very clear about your needs and intent. They can, of course, be more wild and mischievous than you might expect or want. Ask them what they'd like in return for their help ('more chocolate, please!'). Then be ready to open yourself to the energy of these elemental nature spirits. Midsummer's Eve is especially sacred to the faeries and they are more likely than usual to visit us on that night, so you might want to welcome them into your Litha ritual.

Midsummer's Eve is also a time of great magickal power. Re-dedicate yourself to the goals you set out on Imbolc. Give thanks for the progress you've made so far and channel energy into the work yet to be done. As you celebrate your success, you'll find that your enthusiasm for achieving the goals increases. If you have a Litha bonfire, leap over it as you hold your intent in your mind or chant it out loud. Or weave your intent into a flower crown and wear it as a symbol of your work toward your goals.

Be sure to also leave time to relax and enjoy the summer. Litha is a good time for celebrating both work and leisure and, if you have been using the fiery springtime energy to plant, weed and water your spiritual garden, it may be time for a rest. Getting away from your projects for a time can also reinvigorate your dedication to them (that whole 'absence makes the heart grow fonder' thing). Get out into the warm weather for a hike, build some sand castles or play Frisbee. Invite yourself back into the practice of mindfulness, of just being in the moment and enjoying the sensations, without worry or strain.

A balanced combination of work and play, along with the help you'll receive from the faeries, will give your spiritual garden a boost that you'll notice on many levels. Your work on your projects will become more pleasurable and fruitful and, by Lammas, you may notice that the first harvest is even more plentiful than you thought it could be. I wish you patience, faerie energy, joyful toil and productive leisure this Litha!

Litha 2007: The Upward Spiral

Do you ever feel like you're working on the same life lessons over and over again? Often, we find recurring themes in the lessons that appear throughout our lives. It's necessary to keep these recurring challenges in perspective, however. We should recognize the progress we've made along the way, yet acknowledge the places where we need to devote more energy. Our soul work, in my experience, is like an upward spiral.

Sometimes it can be frustrating to see yourself working on 'old' lessons, especially ones you thought you'd learned long ago. One of my own recurring themes is a very Virgoan concern about how others perceive me. To a certain extent, I've shaped my life and career around 'making' other people happy. Now, in my mid-30s, I've come to a hard-earned realization that not only can I not 'make' others happy, but that the best gift I have to give to the world is to be myself and to follow my soul's calling as fully as possible.

I felt that I had released my need to curtail my expressions of self based on others' opinions. Yet that same issue recently came up again in my closest relationships. As I changed my focus, putting more energy into creative projects, my loved ones noticed the change in how I spend my time, and they didn't always appreciate it. I found myself worried about how my loved ones perceived the *ways* I had chosen to pursue my creative work. When I recognized this old pattern recurring, at first I was upset and felt that I was 'right back where I'd started,' but I decided to 'step back' and see the bigger picture.

Often, mentally 'stepping back' and looking at the situation can help us to realize the differences between current and past challenges. In my case, I realized that in the past I would have questioned my entire path, purpose and approach when being challenged or criticized in this way. I realized that I had choices in dealing with the current issues and that they didn't need to be weighted down with old baggage. Instead, I could use the comments to enhance my creative process rather than feel I was 'failing' at it. I could harness the energy of my loved ones, getting them involved in my projects and in the process helping them find their own callings. At this point on the spiral, old negative feelings could inspire new, more creative responses.

Something else that I've found helpful is to be thankful for challenges because they are what help us to learn more about ourselves. Ongoing lessons are like old friends, reminding us of who we once were and helping us learn more about who we're becoming. They also point out areas where we need to focus more attention: 'Yes, you've learned to trust your intuition, but there are still parts of life where you need your logical side.' This can help us to become more balanced and whole individuals.

I often find that the Wheel of the Year corresponds well with the cycle of ongoing lessons. I think back to the previous spring, when similar doubts and fears kept me in bed with a virus for several weeks. Or I call on the fiery energy of last summer to stay focused on my creative pursuits in the face of envy and criticism. Think back to where you were last year at this time and you may find some ready inspiration for your current spiritual work.

As we progress upward along the spiral, we become more adept at seeing these life themes as they arise and taking steps to work through the emotions that they may spark. We become more mindful of our potential weak spots and more thankful for our hard-won strengths. We recover more quickly from our missteps and pitfalls along our path.

So the next time you get the feeling of 'Oh no, not this again,' take some time to gaze back along the spiraling trail, seeing how far you've come. Your journey is what makes you unique and the lessons you've attracted in this lifetime are the ones you've chosen to pursue. Relax into your travels and focus your attention where it is most needed in each moment. Have compassion for yourself, wherever you are in your journey. Blessed Be!

Litha 2008: Creating a Living

When I recently left my longtime employment, my family and friends threw a party for me. Quester lit a bonfire and we gathered around it and offered toasts. Most of my friends, also in their late 30s and early 40s, spoke about how they, too, are pursuing (or planning changes so they can pursue) their callings. My parents, of a different generation, stood and listened, visibly amazed at how we are all leaving mainstream employment to find our own way. They have since been asking questions about how we can 'make a living,' and how we plan to strike out on our own 'in the current economy.'

These questions are good ones, yet they take a somewhat backward approach. Here we are, plunked down in the universe, filled with a variety of desires and preferences. Why would we *not* do what we most want to do? How could we help but manifest the things we need as we pursue our personal paths? What are we here for, anyway?

My partner BlackLion has noticed that many Pagans, while paying positive attention to their spiritual lives, have a conflicted relationship with money. Money itself is not 'wrong' or 'evil.' It is simply a tool, a way to exchange energy. Yet we put limitations on ourselves and maintain old attitudes, particularly that 'making a living' is a difficult thing to do.

Yes, it's true that some people in power have used their tools to perpetuate suffering. Yet the money itself is not to blame. We each know our own ethics and will use all the tools at our disposal to live the best life we can. We are, in fact, always 'creating a living' through our own beliefs and attitudes. If we think it will be tough to earn the money we need to purchase food and shelter, then it will be. If we invest our energy in focusing on our own prosperity, then we'll see our abundance growing.

Rather than focusing on any perceived lack in your life, why not focus on what you *do* enjoy and what you feel grateful for? This will encourage those energies to manifest in your daily life. We often use sympathetic magick in our spells and rituals, knowing that like draws like. This is true with our thoughts, as well. It's not a matter of censoring your doubts or fears, but rather of encouraging your positive visualizations, daydreams and desires.

Do you believe that the divine is loving and kind? That you are a part of nature and belong to the earth? That there is an underlying harmony in the energies of the multiverse? Take a moment to reflect on your underlying spiritual belief system. Now, apply that to your day-to-day life. Are you better off worrying about how to work enough hours to pay the car payment? Or do you focus on what you want (a well-running vehicle to get you where you want to go) and align your thoughts and actions with that goal?

I'm not suggesting you bury your head in the sand and hope the Goddess delivers you some free pizza for dinner. Rather, I'm saying that as you take steps toward your true passions and interests, your path will unfold in a natural way and you will be supported in pursuing your calling. Take this leap of faith and create ways to take small steps towards doing what you love. At the very least, you'll enjoy spending a couple hours a week on a fun hobby. At the most, you'll be surprised how your affinities lead you to a place where you can learn and play even more. You can create an abundant and enjoyable living for yourself and those you love and even have plenty of money to share with the causes you cherish.

What can you do today, right now, to start down this path? Perhaps take some time to focus on the things that you most enjoy. What spells or rituals can you create to help shift your energies? Create a gratitude journal, or charge a coin or other item with your intentions for prosperity. Do you already know what you most want to do or do you want to take time to examine your desires? Maybe meditation will help you to discover and refine your goals. Explore these questions and techniques and create your own. Have fun with the process and let your imagination flower. You might just find your dream job and create a living you may have thought impossible. So mote it be!

Chapter 7

Lammas

Lammas, also called Lughnasadh, is the festival of the first harvest. The God of the Grain is sacrificed to feed the community. The Goddess knows that he will be born once again when the Wheel of the Year turns. Amidst some of the hottest and driest days of summer, we become aware of the coming cold season. The days grow shorter and some crops brown and return to the earth, even as others are still slowly ripening to their full fruition.

Time and memory come to the forefront at Lammas. We notice the seasons begin to shift once again and wonder at how swiftly time passes. What have we been doing with ourselves? How are our projects progressing? We put final touches on the things we wish to harvest and save seeds of other ideas for the next cycle of growth. We get prepared to reap what we've sown.

This Sabbat, even more than the others, may bring ambiguous feelings. We can feel the winds of change beginning to blow. We might wish to slow things down, to have more time to enjoy summer's leisure. Yet we find we must let go and trust the process. As we observe our part in the cycle of life, we are able to sink more deeply into our own spiritual growth, knowing that, like the God, we too will one day return to the earth.

In the meantime, we fulfill our current roles with attention and care. We follow the Threefold Law, work to build healthy communities and learn to live in harmony within our modern culture. We touch the earth gently, feeling her energy through the soles of our bare feet. As priests and priestesses, we keep Books of Shadows, honor rites of passage and see through illusions. We move toward a balance of logic and intuition, trusting that our sensitivity will guide us as the Wheel turns once again.

Lammas 1997: Memory

Last Lammas, I was almost nine months pregnant, weary yet very happy, waiting as patiently as I could for the birth of my son. This summer I have been reminded vividly of that time, not only by his joyful, growing presence, but also by the smell of flowers and cut grass, the late-evening light and the activities of this time of year. That got me thinking about memories and how we store and access them. For example: I can, when I consciously call it up, also remember the excitement and nervousness I felt when I first became pregnant. But that was in winter and the memory does not spontaneously arise as the others do.

Do we, as Pagans or simply as humans, remember events and feelings as part of the earth's natural seasonal cycles? Do the sights and smells and sounds of a particular time of year trigger those memories? I think this is true for many people.

As Pagans, who choose to celebrate the seasons and natural cycles, I think we are more conscious of the link between memory and natural time. As we plan our Sabbat activities and rituals, we remember what we did and how we felt on this holiday in times past. Our record-keeping, in a journal or Book of Shadows, is enhanced by the sensory input we receive from nature.

Since I began to notice this phenomenon recently, I realize that I have also begun to move away from the twelve month calendar-structured memory, to remembering things by the moon's cycles. 'Let's see, when did I last write to my brother? I think it was before last full moon...' Instead of delving for the month and date, it seems easier to mark things by the phase the moon was in.

In pondering why memory, which on the surface seems to be a mental process, is triggered by what surrounds us (smells, sounds, temperatures, etc.), I think of 'cellular memory.' I have encountered the concept in several places, but especially in Jane Roberts' Seth books (an aside: if you have not read any of these,

I highly recommend them. Many of the concepts Seth, a channeled entity, discusses are very compatible with Pagan beliefs. Start with *Seth Speaks*). The body stores events and emotions on a cellular level and can react to them in a very vivid, timeless way. Perhaps when my body smells the summer flowers and feels the warm breezes, I am prompted to remember last summer and the feelings of being stretched tight with new life preparing to burst forth. For you, the same cues could trigger a happy memory of leisurely days by a lake or a painful one of when you broke your leg.

On an individual level, honoring the cycles as well as recalling our experiences within them can help us feel more connected to the earth, to the stories of our own lives and to others in our community ('Remember that Lammas when your cousin from Ireland was here?'). Those of us who keep a journal can, if we don't already, include sensory cues (new moon, awesome thunderstorm, jazz on the radio) which can help us more easily bring events, emotions or rituals to mind much later. And even if you don't bother with written records, you can expect that memories will arise as you need them or you can search the records of your body's awareness.

These ways of remembering and a greater awareness of natural cycles of time seem to be both a return to the way our Pagan ancestors kept track of milestones in their lives and a look ahead to a future when we as a species are more aware of our natural environment and its messages and also the messages of our bodies. Becoming aware of these messages, we can open ourselves to creative ways of remembering and use the knowledge we find there to learn and grow as the Wheel turns once again.

Lammas 1999: Journals

As a solitary witch, it's not always easy to keep track of one's progress along the spiritual path. One good way I've found to gauge my Craft studies over the years is to keep a journal. There are several types of journals that can be helpful.

I must admit to being somewhat of a journal-holic myself (I'm a Virgo. Say no more?). I keep a Tarot journal, with a brief record of the day's events beside the record of the three cards I picked that morning. A cloth-bound blank book holds my thoughts and feelings, as well as significant events. I write in it once a week, on average, and tend to go through one a year. My dream journal records the most significant or memorable of my dreams. Of course, I have my Book of Shadows. And I even participate in a group journal with some close friends from another part of the state.

The daily Tarot journal, which can be adapted for use with runes or other types of divination, is a good way to see how your year is going. At the end of the year, I do a tally of how many times I drew each card (for me, last year was the year of the Page of Swords!). It's also interesting to observe how your day's events match the cards you drew that morning.

My standard journal has served me well in reflecting how I've grown and what I've learned, especially in my metaphysical studies. I read somewhere that there are two rules of journal keeping: 1. Date every entry. 2. Make no other rules. My long-term memory is also not great, so it is valuable as a solitary to be able to refer back to my own reflections. Although I think a journal is of benefit to anyone, since each member of a coven would probably have a different perspective on any given ritual. It might even be fun to 'compare notes' at times.

Most books on dream work suggest keeping a daily dream journal. Personally, I find that I only record dreams when they are particularly vivid or significant to me. Do what seems right for you. But remember, you are the only person who is truly suited to analyze your dreams. Discovering your own personal system of dream symbols is an interesting process, one with which a written record can help.

I find that my personal Book of Shadows is more like a recipe book than a journal. But even so, I go through it every so often to update it and take out things that I no longer need. Being an eclectic, it's all too easy to fill the black ring binder with way too many papers. I find that what I've included can provide insight on what my interests and spiritual needs have been in the recent past ('do I really need 12 prosperity spells?!').

Quester and I keep a group journal with two of our closest friends, a couple who live two hours away. We actually have two notebooks and we exchange them when we see each other (about once a month or so). It's not the only way we keep in touch, but it does provide yet another window on our spirituality and how it is changing and growing. This could be a valuable exercise for a new coven to use to help create the group mind. It could also be useful for an established coven, for example by picking a topic and passing the journal until each member had written about it.

Whatever types of journals you choose, be sure to take time every so often to go back and read what you've written. It can really be an eye-opener and point out to you how far you've come along your chosen path.

Lammas 2000: Where Does the Time Go?

It seems like the summer just arrived and yet it is Lammas, time of the first harvest. For the moment, my family and I are still 'city Pagans,' yet we've been frequenting the farmers' market, camping out as often as we can and enjoying long evening walks. This is the time of year when we start to notice that it's getting dark a little earlier and wonder how high summer went by so quickly.

Not only is Lammas the time for celebration of the first harvest, but it is also time to begin to gear up for the busier harvest season ahead. Even if you don't have a physical farm or garden, it is a time for 'spiritual housecleaning,' to prepare yourself to reap what you have sown and to germinate ideas for your next planting.

Time is one theme of this holiday, as we watch the wheel begin to turn to the dark half of the year once again. It is important to examine what we do with our time and how that reflects our priorities. While the lazy days of summer are still with us, pause and reflect on how best to balance your schedule so that you have time for the people and activities that you hold dear. Don't forget *you*; it is important to nurture yourself, so that you have the energy to share with others.

Take a look at the status of projects and work that you planted this spring. Think back to what you were focusing on earlier in the year; consult your journal if you keep one. Are you ready now to reap the rewards of those plantings? Are they 'ripe' yet? What changes or final touches can you contribute to them as the time draws near?

As you explore your harvest, keep in mind the Threefold Law (and other variations of this idea), which states that what you send out returns to you threefold. In applying this to our creative projects and magickal work, we must realize that we do not set the terms of the return. It might not be what we expected...but it might be what we really need. Or it might take longer than we thought to mature (there's that pesky 'time' factor again).

Remember to save new ideas and projects for the 'second planting.' A friend of mine says that if we have only one goal, we will never achieve it, because some part of our mind then believes that it would have no further purpose and would cease to exist. As you contemplate your spiritual harvest and organize your time, be sure to save seeds of ideas for the next cycle.

If this exercise sounds dull to you, make it fun. At your celebrations of the season, or while sitting by the lake, share your ideas with your friends. Quester gave a favorite recipe to a friend recently and it came back to him in an improved version that he now uses all the time. In the same way, sharing our favorite ideas and projects with those who know us can help us see them from a new perspective. If a project is not going as you expected it would, a coven member might remember how you phrased your wish last Imbolc. An idea for building a labyrinth could become a group endeavor or you might get valuable creative input on your initial design.

As you gear up for the busy season to come (why do I always have a feeling of going back to school, though I've been away from formal education for years now?), organizing your approach to your spiritual path is important. It can help you enjoy your life and your work to the fullest. When you smell autumn in the air and the leaves begin to change color, you may be a little less likely to say 'where does the time go?'

Lammas 2001: The Bridge of Ambiguity

It sounds like the beginning of a bad astrology joke. How do you really piss off a Virgo? Make her learn the lesson of ambiguity. Ambiguity really sucks. I mean, there are some people who truly thrive on it and consider it a big adventure to not know anything about what will happen next. And in certain contexts, I can agree with that perspective. But when one's entire reality starts to melt apart like cheesy visual effects in a movie, it gets annoying.

The previous editor, in her kindness, thanked me for my positive and inspirational words in this column over the past few years and I hope that no one is disappointed by the tone of this note. I'm not trying to whine or complain, just to share the fact that the trickster gods have been pointing and laughing in my general direction lately. And rather than feeling like I can empower others, I've felt rather un-priestess-like and grumpy; alone even in the midst of my community.

I guess the gist of the lesson is best illustrated by the dream I had the other night. I am walking toward a huge old stone bridge. I don't want to cross it, but there is an invisible being (I will call this genderless entity the Guide, for lack of a better word) who is urging me to continue forward. I begin to cross the bridge, under protest. The first third is a narrow paved path along the top of the stonework. The next third, when I reach it, looks impossible to cross. It is the decorative part of this ancient bridge, with loops, intricate stonework and no path at all. I say that I must go back, for there is no way to get across. But the Guide again urges me forward and says that if I hold on with my hands and scale my way across (like a climber on a cliff), my body will be supported. I am terrified, but I trust in the Guide and slowly begin to inch along, supported by invisible hands. At last we make it safely onto the final third of the bridge. Like the beginning, it is a narrow paved path, but it is unfinished, and workers are still paving it and shoring up the stonework. I tell the Guide: 'I'm not supposed to be here. It's not even finished.' My Guide insists that I do belong there and says that I should finish crossing. I edge my way amongst the workers and at last I have crossed this bridge.

That is where the dream ends; I don't know what was on the other side. But just the ambiguous nature of the crossing itself is a metaphor for my current spiritual lessons. To look to the positive, the Guide was indeed there to support and encourage me. In my daily life, I have a supportive circle of friends and family that I turn to. But in a way, that makes these lessons from the underworld of the soul even tougher. I have, to all appearances, everything going for me: a loving community, a new home, a decent job and good health. I can't explain the angst and weirdness of this particular part of my journey. The only thing, and hardest thing, to be done is to let go, to go with the flow and trust that everything happens in its own good time. Forget planning and live in the moment, doing what feels right. I guess we could all use a little more of that in our lives.

Lammas 2002: Creatures of Air

It is still, outwardly, the height of summer as we approach Lughnasadh, but if you listen carefully at this first harvest, you can hear the winds of change beginning to bring autumn our way. Wind, or air, has long been associated with the mind, and with thoughts and ideas. Air is also related to illusions, like that of the endless summer weather and to seeing through those illusions.

As human beings living in the modern world, we are very much creatures of air. In our culture, we tend to over-emphasize this trait, living very much in the world of ideas: books, e-mail, discussions and debates, news updates and financial planning. As an avowed bookworm, I have to say I truly enjoy this realm. Yet, as in all things, balance is necessary.

Thoughts are used, both consciously and unconsciously, to create our reality, the world that we see around us. The 'power of positive thinking' is very real and is directly connected to the element of air. Yet the reverse is also true. If we get into a pattern of negative thinking, we begin to attract negative events in our lives. The 'little black cloud' over our heads begins to set up an undesirable weather pattern. Most of us get into this pattern once in a while or in certain realms of our lives.

To get out of such a pattern, use the power of air to see through illusion. Focus on the good things in your life and let the negativity dissipate like a cloud blown by the wind. This is particularly effective when the problems are truly minor, like car trouble or an outbreak of acne. Yet even with larger issues, you can use the power of air in your rituals, to see through the illusion that you exist only on one plane and to turn your thoughts to a more positive, hopeful view.

Be careful not to fall into the trap of blaming yourself or feeling guilty for your problems. Creating your own reality is not a simple process and we are all here to learn lessons. Guilt only contributes to the negative influence you are working to change. Just because the reasons for your troubles are not simple or clearly visible doesn't mean you are doing something wrong. Pure logic is only part of the picture.

In fact, some of us may try too hard to apply the powers of air to all the aspects of our lives. In particular, this can be a mistake when relating to other people. We use our logic to figure out the motives of others or wonder why two plus two doesn't always make four when talking about relationships. Again, balance is useful. It can help to remember that we are also creatures of water and that emotions can and do overwhelm all of us from time to time. This can exacerbate an argument (the Three of Swords Tarot card comes to mind) when we are trying to refute our loved one's current issues with us point by point, only to have them blow up angrily at us (quite a thunderstorm can result!). Let your voice of logic take a rest and resolve to hear and feel what the other person is truly trying to get across. The person's body language and the tone of voice they use can often be clearer than the content of what they are saying.

Sound is an important tool of air. When dealing with problems, calm yourself by listening to the wind sighing through the trees or rippling the water. Create a mantra or chant that helps with your current situation. It can be an affirmation that has meaning to you, a chant you've used in circle or an ancient sound such as om (aum). Let the sound resonate throughout your mind and your body. The effects can be quite powerful.

Being mindful is another tool you can use to balance your thoughts. Practice existing in the current moment, without letting your thoughts wander into the past or the future. It's helpful to focus on your breath. Feel the air as it flows in and out of your nose and mouth. Let this calm breathing focus you and cleanse your mind. If you are a creature of air, often focusing on thoughts and ideas and letting your mind wander, this practice will be challenging at first. But even the most fruitful minds deserve a break once in a while, so experiment with this technique and see what happens. Take the time to rest and renew yourself before the full onset of the harvest of your ideas and projects.

'May the four winds blow you safely home!'

Lammas 2003: Are You an 'HSP?'

At a recent book sale, I picked up a self-help book about which I'd recently read a magazine article. It's called *The Highly Sensitive Person: How to Thrive When the World Overwhelms You*, and is written by psychologist Elaine N. Aron. Her basic premise is that fifteen to twenty percent of the population has a highly sensitive nervous system. This causes us to become more easily overwhelmed, but also allows us to perceive subtleties that others may miss. It's a neutral trait, yet in our culture a highly sensitive person (HSP) is often seen as flawed: more timid or solitary than 'normal.' In this book, HSPs are encouraged to reframe their life experiences and needs in terms of this trait.

While reading this book, it occurred to me that an unusually large percentage of modern Pagans are probably HSPs ('highly sensitive Pagans!'). HSPs are drawn to look inward and ours is certainly a religion which encourages self-reflection. There are obviously other religions with a similar focus (Buddhism in particular comes to mind), and of course there are many people who are not HSPs who choose this spiritual path. But HSPs seem especially suited to it.

> Because HSPs have such close contact with the unconscious, such vivid dreams, and such an intense pull toward the imaginal and spiritual, we cannot flourish until we are experts on this facet of ourselves (184).

HSPs are often drawn to nature, which has a calming effect. Many are 'fond of reading and quiet study' (81). Both are qualities that many Pagans also display. HSPs also tend to be very creative, which is another common Pagan trait, in my experience.

Seventy percent of HSPs are introverts, which doesn't mean that we dislike people, just that in general we tend to prefer smaller groups and that we tend to protect our inner realities. Paganism is often practiced alone, or in smaller, more intimate groups. It's not often that Pagans assemble in large congregations, such as the ones more common to mainstream churches.

This trait also helps us to focus and concentrate fully, particularly in a safe and familiar environment. The practice of magickal disciplines requires this type of strong concentration and is helped by the ability to notice very subtle sensations. Many HSPs have a very strong intuition and, I would speculate, more highly developed psychic skills in general.

In fact, the author compares HSPs to a class of well-known mages: the 'royal advisors' who, throughout history, with their thoughtful and wise 'priestly' approach, have served to balance the more impulsive and aggressive 'warrior-kings.' She notes that, like Merlin in the King Arthur legends, HSPs often choose vocations where their intuition, thoughtfulness and vision are useful to others. In those roles, we often become respected members of society (or of our circle of friends or workplace).

Finally, many Pagans I've talked to have expressed a feeling of 'not fitting in' as a child or adolescent, which is very common among HSPs. Whether or not you decide to read the book (which has a 'self-test' at the beginning), if the qualities I've described here ring true to you, perhaps it would be helpful to reframe your experience. Instead of feeling negative about either yourself or the less-sensitive people you've encountered who might have judged or hurt you, simply recognize that this trait is a natural part of your being. You can then value the advantages it brings you and take steps to ensure that you don't become too overwhelmed on a daily basis.

Some of the steps suggested in the book, which may seem obvious, are to get enough sleep, take time to relax and 'play' (do things which you truly enjoy), take plenty of time for yourself and meditate or pray often. Exercise and healthy eating will help you keep your balance, too. Most important, when you need to remove yourself from an over-stimulating situation, do so without self-recrimination, knowing that your needs are healthy and valid. Taking care of yourself in these ways will help you to better serve the gods and the community as the powerful priestess or priest that you are.

Lammas 2005: Healthy Communities

What does the word 'community' mean to you? In earlier times, it would have meant the family and neighbors who lived near you. You would have relied on each other to help provide food and shelter throughout the year. Most of the families probably would have worshipped together and shared the same basic value system. At this time of the year, you'd be working together to gather the first harvest and keep the rest of the crops watered and weed-free.

These days, community may mean that same physical community of neighbors, but you may also think of your intentional community, those with whom you choose to spend time because of common interests and beliefs. These communities of choice can create healthy opportunities to interact with others in a comfortable way. But chances are that you belong to several communities: your coven and the Maine Pagan community, but also your colleagues at work, people who pursue the same hobby (such as a musical group or chorus) or groups of people who do volunteer work.

If you have children, you've probably also found yourself involved in a community because of them, through school or their other activities. As homeschoolers, my family has for the most part been free to choose other homeschool families with common interests with whom to create community. But my son's recent interest in team sports (yep, I'm a soccer mom) has gotten us involved in a group of families in our town. Many different types of people all get together to support their kids as they learn to play together as a team. I like the diversity of being a part of groups I wouldn't necessarily choose to hang out with. I'm finding I really enjoy being an 'ambassador of the freaks' to the mainstream community ('well, they don't eat meat or send their kids to school, but they seem to be a nice family').

You may or may not choose to be open about being Pagan within some of these groups, but nevertheless you bring your beliefs and ethics with you wherever you go. How do you see your place in your communities? How can you make each community a healthy and productive place to spend time? You may be the one who makes sure the group follows earth-friendly practices, like recycling. Or perhaps you've introduced the concept of consensus to a volunteer group that's having trouble agreeing on a plan of action. Maybe, like me, you're the parent who brings healthy snacks when it's your turn to feed a group of eight and nine-year-olds.

As a person actively pursuing a spiritual path, rest assured that your wisdom will be sought. I've noticed that people are often drawn to Pagan clergy members, even when they have no conscious knowledge of that role. After the events of September 11, 2001, I found myself involved in discussions, at work and elsewhere, with people who were looking to me for reassurance and help making sense of the tragic events. It was a service I was happy to provide, while at the same time I found it amusing to be consulted in a priestess capacity by Christians and atheists.

No matter which communities you're involved with, it's important to be true to yourself and your path as you interact with others. As Pagans we don't proselytize, but neither should we subsume our beliefs in order to go along with the crowd. If you just be yourself, politely and diplomatically, you'll gain far more respect than if you're aggressive about your way being 'the only right way,' or than if you constantly change your actions in order to blend in with those of other community members. Being in community is certainly a lot of work, but it can also be very rewarding, as you find that others are there for you when you need support, just as you are for them.

Lammas 2006: Barefoot Hiking

Last summer at a Reclaiming Witch Camp, I (re)discovered the joys of going barefoot. It was a very rainy week and the terrain was hilly, rocky and muddy. Soon all three of the pairs of shoes I had brought (sandals, sneakers and hiking boots) were completely soaked through and the notion of dry socks was a laughing matter. So, I decided to go barefoot. My studies that week were focused on connecting with nature and the divine and I soon found that having my skin directly connected to the earth with each step was a profound experience. By the time I came home, I could hardly wear shoes at all. The chakras on the bottom of my feet were wide open and the energy between myself and Mother Earth was flowing freely.

Over time, as the weather grew colder and wetter, I forgot about going barefoot. During the winter, I resumed wearing socks and shoes and wore slippers in the house so that my feet would stay warm. I ordered some new Birkenstocks online, thinking ahead to spring, not recalling the way my feet felt on the cool grass. Spring came and it was rainy and cool, so I stayed with socks and close-toed shoes. But, at last, the sun peeked through and I started hiking.

Not wanting to get my new Birks muddy on a hike with Quester, I decided to take them off and put them in my backpack. Within moments, I could feel the energy of the forest more strongly: the trees breathing, the earth's heartbeat, the life force of the moss and flowers, the humbling strength of the rocks. My awareness continued to expand as I walked, placing each foot as if in a moving meditation. As my consciousness shifted, colors seemed brighter, my love and joy for Quester seemed bigger and I could feel the attention of the Goddess upon me. Barefoot hiking made a beautiful day even more magickal and meaningful.

Recently I was able to introduce BlackLion to the pleasures of barefoot hiking. Getting past the initial discomfort of roots and sharp stones, he opened himself to the experience, as I had done at Witch Camp. I could see the shift in his consciousness as he allowed the direct connection with the earth to flow up through his feet. We also did some silent hiking, which again expanded our awareness of the energies surrounding us and connecting us. The cool mud soothed our feet and we headed for low spots on the trail, rather than going around them. Flat rocks in the sun also became favorite spots for a moment of rest and we picnicked with our feet in the stream, feeling ourselves fully open to all of the elements: cold water, hot sun, soothing breeze and patient rocks.

The reaction of the other hikers was interesting and amusing. Most people were incredulous that we would hike barefoot and said things like, 'You must have really tough feet!' One woman said she 'could never do that,' to which BlackLion quipped, 'Sure you could, just take off your shoes.' A little girl told him intently, 'You have mud on your feet.' An older woman stopped us to tell us about a friend of hers who always hiked barefoot and who had written a philosophical treatise about the benefits. That led me to do a little bit of research when I got home and I found a cool website, http://www.barefooters.org/hikers, that will give you more information if you're interested.

Hiking has long been one of my favorite summer activities and now it has taken on a new dimension, directly related to the energy work I've been doing. Go ahead and try it, with a friend or on your own. Or if you don't hike, take a barefoot walk around your yard or a park. Open yourself to the loving energies of the earth, grounding and releasing with each deliberate step. Enjoy the warmth and aliveness of the earth at this vibrant time of the year. Blessed Lammas!

Lammas 2009: The Spiral of Spiritual Growth

As Pagans, we observe and celebrate the notion of cycles: the seasons, the phases of the moon, the lifecycles of humans, animals and other creatures. I've observed that our own process of spiritual growth also tends to move in a cyclical manner. As we travel along our path, we move through stages along the way, each marking a particular terrain with its own unique features.

We each begin in a place of seeking, looking first outside of ourselves, then peering within for answers. We find our chosen tools, honing our skills through practice. We then realize that what we sought was within us all along. And, finally, we turn outward once again, sharing our wisdom with our communities. We may travel this circle, or perhaps it is more accurately described as an upward spiral, many revolutions throughout our lives. Or we might pause in one of these roles, either enjoying what we learn there or perhaps feeling a bit stuck, until we reach out (or in) once again and begin to move. If we get stuck, we might move on from where we are, or perhaps start over, seeking new answers for our current questions.

In thinking about these five stages of spiritual progress, I've come up with the following descriptions and suggestions. Each step has both positive and negative aspects, which I've described below. When you read them, notice if any of them resonate with you; this might be a clue to where you are currently residing on the spiral. I've also included some suggestions about how to encourage the positive aspects and overcome the negative aspects of each stage and to help regain your spiritual momentum if you feel stagnant.

As you read, also remember that you are where you are supposed to be. All is well, so there is nothing to 'fix.' Our growth will lead us ever onward, exploring this incarnation here on earth and finding new things to learn and enjoy. All of the roles described here work together in harmony. We need experienced teachers in our community, yet we also need brand-new seekers who are looking for their knowledge. We need people who are out in the world, taking action, as well as folks who are holding a contemplative and meditative space.

Here are the phases of spiritual growth as I currently perceive them. Please feel free to add your own wisdom and adapt it to your own experience.

Seeking

As our lives become more hectic and hurried, more fragmented and isolated, we long for something without knowing what it is. – from *The Twelve Wild Swans* by Starhawk and Hilary Valentine

The place of seeking begins with a longing for answers. We begin to explore the realm of the spirit, perhaps reading books or attending workshops. We seek out a teacher or religion. Looking outside ourselves, we study the wisdom and knowledge that other seekers have left behind.

We might find what we are looking for right away, perhaps in an existing religion or tradition. We find a coven that is just the right fit for us and begin training with them. Or our search may lead us over numerous hills and through many valleys, the answers we find inspiring further questions. That which we seek seems to be just over the next hill.

The negative, or shadow side, of seeking is that we may become perpetual students. Either we absorb some of the teachings and then move on, never content to delve deeply into a particular source of wisdom, or perhaps we continue to study one area so intently that our life becomes imbalanced. We are so focused on the seeking itself that we never allow ourselves to come to any conclusions about what we believe. In order to avoid being stuck in this mode, you might devote yourself to a particular set of teachings for a year and a day. If you are studying on your own, write an article or research paper that encompasses what you've been learning. These actions will help you shift from a mode of constant movement and passive receiving into a place of more depth and active sharing.

The positive part of seeking is the innocence of the beginner's mind. In yoga, we are encouraged to approach each pose, or asana, as if it is the first time we have practiced it. This keeps the mind on the present moment. If we are truly seeking and open to finding wisdom, we are never jaded or cynical. We are able to take in that which we see, fully and with an open mind and heart. By practicing mindfulness, or being fully in the moment, no matter what task you are involved in, you can cultivate this sense of innocence and wonder.

The phase of seeking, as we begin to evaluate what we've found, naturally leads to the second stage, that of:

Contemplation

Know that your seeking and yearning will avail you not, unless you know the Mystery: for if that which you seek, you find not within yourself, you will never find it without. – from The Charge of the Goddess by Doreen Valiente

The next phase of spiritual growth involves going deeply within oneself. We turn inward and discover a marvelous world of thoughts, ideas, feelings and dreams. We take time to meditate and find our own unique voice. Realizing that our own experience is valid and valuable, we take the time to explore our inner being.

To some people, the place of contemplation comes naturally. For others, it may seem scary at first. In our modern society, we are not encouraged to be alone with our thoughts. Allowing ourselves true quiet, unstructured time can be an amazing gift. We begin to explore our own gifts of creativity and find the things we most enjoy.

The shadow side of contemplation can be isolation and over-analysis. We may, like a hermit, draw apart from the daily activity of the world. While this is valuable to do, taken to the extreme it can become a lonely place. If we are constantly philosophizing and analyzing our inner experiences, we can forget to live, to enjoy the simple pleasures life offers us. As an antidote to being stuck in that mode, remember that having a social network is healthy. You don't need to become a social butterfly, but having a few friends to get together with on a regular basis is a fun and interesting part of life, and all the more so if you can relate to them on a spiritual level.

Being in a space of contemplation has many positive aspects. We are each unique and a deeper understanding of our own thoughts and ideas benefits everyone. Even if we choose to keep our discoveries to ourselves, the energy that we radiate will shine out into the universe. Contemplation often leads us to capturing our ideas in writing, music or other compositions. That which we create will be well thought out and will radiate our depth. To encourage your inner exploration, purposefully set aside time to accomplish it. If you were attending rituals and classes, those times would show up in your calendar. Do the same for yourself and schedule blocks of time when you can simply be, without having to do anything in particular.

Once you have charted the terrain of your inner world, the next phase is:

Practice

Religions don't exist within theories and ritual plans; they come to life only when they're being practiced and lived. – from *Living Wicca* by Scott Cunningham

Now is the time when we take the tools that we've learned through seeking and contemplating and work with them as we travel along the path. This is a lively phase, when we focus on skill-building and taking action in the world. We are really 'walking the walk,' living our spiritual ethics on a daily basis. We choose to do the things that will help us achieve our goals and our purpose on the earth.

We might become active in causes that are deeply important

to us, from environmental justice to helping feed the hungry. We pursue our calling, perhaps by changing careers or starting a coven or other spiritual group. We are the ones who show up for volunteer days or take notes at meetings. A regular practice of meditation, yoga or prayer is formed and nurtured. Our spiritual fire sustains us as we continue to show up in meaningful ways.

The downside of practice is that we can burn ourselves out. We are constantly on the go, always busy, never slowing down. Unless we pause to nurture our bodies and spirits, we won't be able to keep up this pace for long. To make sure you have enough energy to do all of these important things, be consistent about taking 'down time' for yourself. Turn off the phone for the evening, grab a good book and take a long bubble bath. Do this more than once a year.

The blessings of practice are that we are able to master those things we love. We are also able to contribute to the world in a meaningful way. We make connections, build community, take action to make changes. Our society expands as we bring this new energy to it. We reach our goals and then set new ones. We work with others of like mind. One way to encourage yourself in this work is to write, or at least formulate mentally, a personal mission statement. This is a statement of your deepest values and spiritual goals, summed up in a sentence or two. Then, once you've written it, revise it once each year, perhaps at Imbolc. Post it on your bulletin board or computer desktop, so you'll be reminded why you do what you do.

As practice becomes mastery, our confidence expands and leads to the state of:

Awakening

The real reason you chose to be here – your purpose and mission in life – was to simply be who you are now. Good reason. – from *Notes From the Universe* by Mike Dooley

At some point, we become a bit weary of our constant activity. We are drawn inward once again and long to find an even deeper meaning to our lives. In the course of this process, we come to an epiphany. While it is different for each of us, the essence is a recognition of our own wisdom and perfection. It is a feeling of 'I'm already there!' Our striving and reaching ceases and we understand that just being ourselves is truly enough.

The drive to seek and to do recedes and we are powered by the sheer joy of life. We focus on discovering anew all those things that we truly love, not as a way to get somewhere else, but for fun. This stage is full of self-discovery, but in a much more relaxed way. We may study, contemplate and practice what we are discovering, but we do so in a more conscious way than before. We are awakening to our true nature.

The danger of this stage lies in thinking that our way is The Way. If we start thinking like this, we may try to convert others to our path and push our truth onto them. We become evangelists for our own flavor of spirituality. Remember that everyone will eventually come to discover those things that are their personal truths. Yes, as humans, some of these will be in common, but it's not your job to drag others up the mountain. Remind yourself of this whenever you're tempted to give an impromptu lecture or sermon.

On the positive side, awakening brings our powers of creativity to new heights. We discover that not only can we create a poem or quilt or garage, but that we are creating our entire experience. We are flourishing as we live our life's purpose. Even when we experience challenges, we see them as an important part of the process of our lives. As you explore this phase of your spiritual growth, support yourself by purposefully surrounding yourself with positive voices, images and media. The mass culture worships negativity and bad news. To avoid getting distracted and dragged down, listen to inspiring speakers, play beautiful music and plant flowers. Enjoy being in nature and playing in the elements.

Our awakening brings to us a fullness of spirit, a light that overflows our own lives and leads us to the stage of:

Teaching

The master's task is to teach us to receive, without any obscurations of any kind, the clear message of our own inner teacher, and to bring us to realize the continual presence of this ultimate teacher within us. – from *The Tibetan Book of Living and Dying* by Sogyal Rinpoche

Now we turn outward once more and share our wisdom with the community. At any of the stages described above, we can decide to teach what we know. This phase, however, is where we embody the archetype of an elder or wise one. Our teachings are genuine and open and come from a place of wanting to share with those who are truly interested in what we have to offer.

We might never lead a workshop or teach a class, but simply teach by being. We are living our own purpose and our joy radiates outward to others as we move through the world. The very act of following our calling, of living our spirituality, begins to change things and people, wherever we go. Now we are a spiritual master; which is not to say that we are perfect, for we are still human. But we have realized our own version of enlightenment and can share that energy with the earth and all her beings.

Of course, we will still have an ego, and the shadow side of this phase is becoming addicted to the respect and adoration we may receive. There are numerous stories of the guru who takes advantage of his or her disciples. The way to avoid this is to remain grounded. Wash your own dishes, work in the garden, go places where no one knows who you are. Continue to do things by yourself, taking time to stay active in exploring your truths.

The positive side of being a teacher includes not only the benefit to our students, but also the feedback and inspiration we receive from our interactions with them. We teach that which we need to know, so often we receive as much from our chosen lessons as our pupils will. To encourage this sharing of energy, it can help to practice when to speak and when to remain silent. Active listening is an important skill as a teacher or role model. Often those we interact with simply want to be truly heard. Those who seek us out have been inspired to do so from their own deep longing, so observe their actions and words as a source of new knowledge. They, and we, are parts of the universe wanting to know itself better.

As we move up the spiral, traveling through these five stages, our sense of personal responsibility for our own lives increases. We teach our own wisdom and then we move on, seeking new vistas from which to view the world. Like The Fool card in the Tarot, we begin anew, starting over with a fresh beginner's mind, yet containing all the wisdom of all that we have explored, in this life and others.

Chapter 8

Mabon

Mabon is the time of the Autumnal Equinox, when once again the days and nights are in balance. This time, the wheel is turning towards the darkness and cold of winter. We feel the urge to balance our own dualities and learn to keep this delicate balance once we've found it. Like our ancestors, our thoughts turn toward preparing for the cold months to come. We seek ways to (literally and metaphorically) store our harvests for future use. We use the sunny, cool days as fully as possible, finding many ways to be productive.

Life itself is a creative endeavor. This becomes quite evident in autumn, when the bounty of the earth surrounds us. We are the creators of our own life experiences. As our awareness of our power-from-within expands, we honor our changing needs. We are learning that the value is in the journey, not the destination. At Mabon, even during the busiest days of harvest time, we begin turning toward quiet reflection and inner journeying. We devote more time to our projects, expressing the ideas we've been nourishing all throughout the growing season. Our personal spiritual symbols serve to remind us of the lessons we've been integrating.

We check in once more with the priorities and goals that we set out for the year. Seeing how the days grow ever shorter, we choose our activities more carefully. The energies of the harvest begin to wind down and we look to what sustains us. Perhaps we are stepping into a new leadership role, becoming openly Pagan in our communities or transforming ourselves once again and gaining confidence along the way. We might find ourselves questioning where we are and making course corrections. Again and again, we choose love and joy along the path. As we evaluate what we're harvesting this season, we tuck away inspiring ideas that we'll use in our creations during the long, dark winter.

Mabon 1997: Pagans in the Community

There is a bumper sticker that I've always liked that says 'There Are More of Us Than You Think.' In reflecting on Pagans in the community in Maine and New England, it seems to me to be a very true statement.

Over the summer I encounter more Pagans (outside of my circle of family and friends) than at any other time of the year, probably due to the warm weather and the outdoor events being held around the state. I attend what I call 'open-minded' fairs that take place each year: WERU's Full Circle Summer Fair, the Maine Festival and the Common Ground Country Fair. There I see many Pagans, as well as like-minded folks (like my Mom, a 'natural Pagan' who considers herself agnostic yet believes in reincarnation and the power of the earth and who taught me a system of ethics that I later discovered parallels most Pagan faiths). Also at the fairs, I find Pagans doing outreach to the local community, such as the folks who staff the EarthTides booth and give lectures on Wicca (my thanks to all of you!). In the summer, too, I get out and walk more. I often see houses with bountiful herb gardens and stars-and-moon decorations and I wonder...

At other times of the year, however, and in the mainstream media, Pagans usually tend to fade into the background. An exception is around Samhain (Halloween), when the local press tries to locate and interview a 'real' witch. But why are we not generally recognized as members of a legitimate religion? There are a few reasons.

Some might say it's because of the members of Christian community, some of whom fear Pagans and think of us as devil-worshippers. But here in Maine, although some prejudice certainly exists, I think ignorance is a more common factor. Many people in the general public simply don't know much about

Pagans or Wiccans. They think of witches as characters in movies or fairy tales, or know about us only on the periphery of their experience (like Deadheads, who used to get press only when the band was in town, but who were and are part of life in Maine).

Another reason, which also contributes to why people are ignorant of our beliefs, is the highly individual, close-knit nature of Pagans. I generally think that this is a good thing, since one's belief system is very personalized. We don't try to convert others to our faith, nor should we. But the way most Pagans feel about being part of any organized system can also work to our disadvantage, when the work that we do in the community is not seen as part of our Pagan life-path.

For example, many Pagans I know work in very ethical, caring professions. Pagans are nurses, social workers, healers, environmentalists and teachers. But in their work lives, they might not talk about or openly display their Pagan faith (sometimes a necessary precaution for keeping the job). Many Pagans also do volunteer work or offer help to those they encounter who are in need. This is not often done as overtly Pagan work (with exceptions of course, like the great work being done by the Pagan Pantry in the Bangor area).

The most important thing, of course, is that the work is being done. But I for one would like to see more awareness of the Pagan contribution to the community. How can we help create this awareness? I think the new direction being taken by EarthTides is on track; I'm curious about what will happen in the next few months and I hope many people will participate. Another development, which I only have enough space (and experience) to touch on here, is the Pagan community's use of the Internet. From e-mail lists to chat rooms to web pages, the anonymity and often easy access to the internet is encouraging many folks to get in touch.

We as Pagans also need to speak up in public about who we are and what we believe in (easier said than done). People are less likely to discriminate against those they can see and recognize as productive members of the community.

Mabon 1999: Stepping Into the Priestesshood

As a solitary Pagan for many years, I longed to have a spiritual community, to join a coven like the ones I read about. I wanted to be taught by an elder of the Craft. Being shy didn't help my search for community. So I made my own vows to the Goddess and the God in a self-dedication ritual and went on with my studies.

But there were many times when I doubted my own abilities and once again wished for teachers and colleagues. My longing for a group was increased by my growing awareness that I had been part of an active community of witches in at least one previous life and by dreams of circle meetings in a cozy book-lined living room filled with friends I hadn't met in waking life (yet).

So I read Starhawk's *Dreaming the Dark* and tried to start a spiritual discussion group with some friends and acquaintances. It lasted only a short time, torn apart by some members' jealousy of new friendships being formed among others in the group. This hurt. I withdrew back into my solitary practice for a long time after that, viewing it as a 'failed experiment.'

Over the next few years, Quester and I did some ritual work with some friends of ours. I learned from them and they insisted that they learned a lot from me about witchcraft and magick. I was glad, but didn't consider it a coven, since not all the members considered themselves witches (at least initially), our celebrations weren't regular and we didn't follow a specific mythos. Other Pagans began to come to me for advice, seeing me as a leader and teacher. I tried to help as much as I could, but always in the back of my mind was 'if only I had a real priestess to consult.'

Those of you who have practiced as a solitary for a long time may see where this is going. Within the past year, a friend and I began talking about starting a circle. Once again doubting my experience, I suggested we seek out a teacher, or at least someone to consult with on how covens are formed. But that search was not successful, for I needed to learn and assimilate the lesson the Goddess kept presenting to me: to trust myself and what I had learned.

I still feel there is tremendous value in being trained and initiated by an established coven. But, as a solitary witch of several years, I needed to let go of my preconceptions and step into the role of priestess. We are not a religion of large congregations and a select priesthood, but quite the opposite. We can all work directly with the gods. You will know when you have been initiated into Her service, no matter how formal or informal the experience. Trust the divine within and you will in time take your place as a priest or priestess of the Craft (and maybe sooner than you think). This is true whether or not you desire to work with others.

We started our circle this spring and now at harvest it is ripening into a supportive, magickal working group. Be patient, and when the time is right, your spiritual community will come to be. And you may, like me, be right up there in front of the altar, leading the very first ritual. Blessed Be!

Mabon 2000: Symbols

What are your personal spiritual symbols? Christians share the cross as a symbol and many Pagans identify with the pentacle. But go deeper, into your own spiritual life, the omens you regard as significant, the feelings you experience when you walk between the worlds. Are there symbols that you hold dear?

The problem with describing transcendent spiritual experiences is that words are inadequate to explain how one's world is transfigured. The moment may pass in the blink of an eye, yet linger for eons in your soul. From day to day, we may forget how we have been transformed...but where words fail, symbols can trigger our memories, delivering us back into a powerful moment.

Such a symbol need not be visual. The echoing chime of a set of Tibetan bells or the smell of a heavy rain, may set us alight. For me, a sensation of spinning, often while sitting still in meditation, carries me away to time outside of time. Symbols can be living beings: a favorite maple, as its leaves become brilliant orange and gold, may remind you of the sacred turning of the Wheel of the Year.

Most of these symbols come to us unbidden, as gifts of the universe and of our own unique psyches. But at those times when the world seems faded, when you may doubt your power-from within, you can use personal symbols as triggers to shift your awareness. Put on a recording of your favorite Goddess chants or burn incense that you have used in circle. Read the Charge of the Goddess aloud, for words too can be symbols. Let your creativity flow; paint, draw or drum your favorite symbols.

If nothing comes to mind as a personal symbol, explore your own physical landscape. What kind of artwork are you drawn to? How does your clothing reflect your inner self? What songs play in your head as you walk? Allow symbols to enter your life. Make space for them to come to you and pay attention to what unfolds.

Working with the Tarot or other divination systems is one way to allow archetypal symbols to become personal. Choose a deck that brings you pleasure and find the cards that evoke strong sensations. Use your intuition to discern what they mean to you and you may be surprised at how the images become part of your life. Different cards will cycle through your awareness at different times. For an entire year, the Daughter (Page) of Swords from the Motherpeace deck was part of almost every reading I did for myself. As I integrated her energies and lessons, I drew the card less often. But when I need to draw on those energies now, I can meditate on the card or simply call up its image in my mind, as a symbol to trigger my awareness.

Experiment with your personal spiritual symbols and remember to honor their gift with a prayer or offering. You will find that symbols can help to enrich your spiritual practice and can serve as an invaluable reminder, during the 'dark times of the soul,' of your connection to the Web of Life.

Mabon 2001: The Flow of Creative Energy

What is it about this time of year that appeals so strongly to my creativity? Even more than in the spring, when fertility and active creation is all around, it is during leaf-fall that my juices flow and I come up with loads of ideas for projects and work I want to do. An easy answer is the old pattern of 'back to school,' but I think there is a deeper answer.

This turn of the Wheel is when the gardens and fields are full of the manifestations of an earlier idea, once contained in a seed. The trees show their brightest, most delightful colors. The fruitfulness (literally) of life is evident. As the days get shorter and the golden evenings darken more quickly, we, like the other animals, feel the need to prepare for the turning-inward of winter. These days, as many of us have grown away from the old ways of preparing for the cold and dark, and do less of the necessary, survival-oriented work of our ancestors, the way that we prepare for the darker time is to express, onto paper or canvas or in our other projects, some of the ideas we've been nourishing through the summer. To return, with new energy, to work that we might have lain aside. Honoring these rhythms within ourselves, the urge to rapidly create and do and prepare, can be part of our growth.

I have written before about the 'winter holiday' season and how its frenzied pace goes against a natural inclination to slow down and look within. Part of the enjoyment and satisfaction of slowing our pace once winter begins can come from having had a 'productive' autumn.

Nurturing your impulse to create without scattering your energies in too many directions can be challenging. As always, I recommend keeping a personal journal, a place where you can jot down or sketch any new ideas or elaborations on current projects. This will help you capture important inspirations without having to hold them all in your head (mine tend to bounce around in there and start echoing, which can be annoying).

Having your priorities and goals in mind, or better yet, on paper in your Book of Shadows, can keep you on track. Rather than saying a hasty 'yes' to a friend's request for help with starting an intriguing new discussion group, you can remember the fact that you're still working on designing your circle's next ritual, as well as organizing a charity event and editing some poetry, and decline or postpone your involvement in a new project.

And the practice of some sort of reflective time, such as meditation or mindfulness, can remind you that the value of the things you pursue is in the doing, not in the end result. My family is known for craft projects that are started and left undone for years, but the notion of their value being in the experience and pleasure of working on them can stop the judging mind in its tracks. And some fall, years hence, you might pick up that embroidery project or wood carving and be inspired to finish it as the perfect gift for a new friend.

Although it sounds like I'm encouraging you to be busy this fall, I urge you to spend your energy and time on projects that feed your soul. Don't do anything simply because you feel you 'should,' or because you 'have always done it.' Open to the flow of creative energy that emanates naturally through you and let it take you where you truly want to go. Sniff the crisp air, taste the fresh crisp vegetables and let yourself fall into your work with true joy and enthusiasm.

Mabon 2002: A Quest for Balance

One of the key features of many Pagan religions is duality, and more specifically, the balance of that duality. The Goddess and the God dance in and out of balance over the Wheel of the Year, as we humans do throughout our lives. There are many dualities that we hold in balance: male and female energies, logic and intuition, work and play, extroversion and introversion, reverence and mirth, joy and sorrow, positive and negative, light and shadow, active and passive, health and illness, change and stability, to name only a few.

As the Autumnal Equinox, a time of balance between night and day, approaches, I've been musing on balance and how to achieve it, or more accurately, how to recognize it. I am fortunate to have several people in my life whose sun sign is Libra, the sign of balance (and my own moon is in Libra, as well). My friends and I joke that there are two types of Librans: those who strive meticulously to remain in balance at all times and those who find balance over time by careening between the extremes. I think that, as human beings, it is futile to expect that we will always be in perfect balance. It is a beautiful goal to aim for, but if we don't allow ourselves to rock from one side of the scales to the other, we'll become stressed out when we do fall out of balance.

Take, for example, the balance between rest and activity. Cycles are such that there will be times when we find ourselves busy and on the go: a busy month, season or even a year when we seem to get less rest than usual. But if you look back at the big picture, you'll often see that there have been times when you have had periods of rest and leisure, whether you've created them purposefully or they have naturally emerged.

I believe that balance naturally surrounds us, if we can only recognize it. Another example: you are trying to eat a balanced diet. On the day you are thinking about it, you realize you've had plenty of fruit, vegetables and grains, but no protein. Yet if you think back over the previous week, you find that you had plenty of protein leading up to this moment. It is when we focus in on the details that we lament our lack of balance, yet over time it often tends to even out.

And when that is not true, when some aspect of our lives has been one-sided for a long time, a crisis will often arise. Whether it is conscious or not, we know when something is missing, when a change is needed. That's when an illness or injury forces us to slow down, a relationship ends and spurs us to re-evaluate our needs and desires or some other unmistakable 'wake-up call' appears in front of us.

I think one of the keys to finding balance over time is allowing yourself to change and grow. If you have a set view of yourself which remains rigid over the years, you are blocking your own natural cycles. Sure, perhaps you've always been a person who feels happier surrounded by people and worshipping in a large circle, but maybe now you need some time alone to reflect and do more solitary magick. It's natural for your personality and needs to change over time.

It also helps to have supportive people around you, who will allow you to change without trying to hold you back. I'm always amazed by people who have been divorced lamenting, 'She wasn't the same person I married ten years ago.' Why do we expect others to remain stagnant, even as we are growing and learning? We do them a disservice with that kind of attitude. Be sure the members of your circle of friends are understanding of the process of growth and then seek their advice when you stumble on the path.

Old aspects must die away to make room for the new ones to emerge, so that we may find balance as we journey through a lifetime. The growth process often makes the road seem bumpy for a while, but be patient with yourself as you travel. If you notice some aspect of your life that seems out of balance, do some introspection about why that might be so and whether it is actually balancing other aspects over time. Then focus on how you might adjust it, if you feel the need. Don't rebuke yourself for your momentary glitches, as long as you continue to grow. Remember to step back and get a bigger view. Good luck to you on your quest for balance.

Mabon 2003: Keeping Your Balance

The Fall Equinox is upon us, when the days and nights are of equal length. The Wheel of the Year is poised to turn towards the darkness, when the days dwindle in length until the Winter Solstice. At this moment in time, there is balance. How is balance reflected in your life?

There are many ways to interpret that question: balancing work with recreation, rest with activity, spirituality with mundane-world actions, eating a balanced diet, balancing family and social time with time to be alone, balancing your finances, and many others I'm sure you can think of.

I recently heard an interview with Dr. Joan Borysenko and she made the point that even trying to achieve balance can be stressful, if we think we have to balance everything every day or week 'Gee, I have to have time this morning to meditate and do my yoga, then I'm off to work, running errands, dinner with the family, then circle...no time to get some cardiovascular exercise, and when will I call my best friend?' She suggested that we understand that we'll have busy times, as well as times when things are quieter, and as such, we should look at the balance of our lives over time.

As Pagans, we might do well to let our balance flow with the natural and agricultural cycles of the earth. Right now we're in 'harvest mode.' The earth's bounty is being gathered from the fields before the frosts begin and preparations are being made for the winter to come. This might be reflected in our lives in practical ways, like winterizing the home, or in less tangible ways, such as organizing your calendar for the next few weeks or gathering in energy from your spiritual harvest of lessons you've learned. Once the frosts come and the days get even shorter, the leaves begin to fall from the trees and the last of the flowers fade. We might begin to allow ourselves more quiet restful time or gather our friends for small dinner parties rather than boisterous celebrations. It's a good time for reflection and for inner journeying.

We can, of course, also balance our actions and energies with the lunar cycles. Many of us do this naturally, especially women, whose monthly menstrual cycle can remind us (sometimes quite forcefully!) of when we need to rest. But if you feel a lack of balance in your life, start paying more attention than usual to the phases of the moon. Schedule your most active days for the waxing moon, allowing yourself more time to rest when the moon is waning and taking time to be alone during the dark of the moon. See how that feels for you; some people have more energy when the moon is new and others when it is full.

If you still feel off-balance in your life, then drop activities if you're too busy or add new ones if you feel your life is too dull or routine. This might sound like simple advice, but many of us maintain social or community activities that no longer sustain us, becoming too busy as we add the new things that we're excited about. Let go of guilt, and if you don't want to do something, decide to drop it, or at least to approach it differently. Know that you can say 'No thank you' when you receive invitations. Similarly, if we feel a lack of community and wish to be more involved, sometimes we find it easier to complain than to actually get out in the world and make new connections. Don't let yourself put it off; learn a new hobby, take a class or attend a public ritual.

Take time this fall to reflect on your own life and how you feel about its balance. You might discover ways to become even more in tune with the earth's cycles, which in turn will help you have more energy as you walk your path.

Mabon 2004: A Harvest of Creativity

As fall begins, all around us we can see the fruits of Mother Earth's creativity. Apples, pumpkins, zucchini, corn and tomatoes are abundant. We human beings are by nature creative beings, tending the soil to help coax forth an ample harvest of food, as well as beautiful flower gardens to enhance our surroundings.

We also create art: from music to quilting to creative writing; from painting to dancing to carpentry. Even those who don't consider themselves artists in the traditional sense are creative beings. On a fundamental level, we create the lives that we live, to a greater or lesser extent depending on our beliefs. We set and work toward goals, we react to events, we use our focused intent to attain the results we desire. Living is a creative endeavor.

The fall, with its feeling of quickening activity as we leave behind the 'lazy, hazy days of summer' and begin to prepare for the coming cold season, is a good time to focus on our own expressions of creativity. There are many ways to allow new ideas to inspire us and encourage our creative work. Here are a few, which I offer with the hope that they might spark further thoughts for you to explore:

- **Nature.** Let the natural world infuse your imagination. Walking in the woods, working in the garden or gazing at the mountains in the distance can encourage a break-through on a tricky project. Or it can simply relax you enough to allow new ideas to surface.
- **Dreams.** Dream imagery is rich in creativity. Many of the world's famous artists and scientists found inspiration while they slept. Take time when you wake each morning to remember your dreams and ponder what messages they are delivering.
- **Daydreams.** Repetitive tasks, such as hanging out laundry, doing dishes or driving, can allow part of the mind to wander. Solutions to problems can suddenly surface or you

may find yourself viewing things in a new way. If you're alert, you may be able to capture some of the essence of the daydream and use it in your projects (though if you are driving, be sure to keep at least some of your focus on the road!).

- **Personal experience.** Your life experiences, your times of joy and of adversity, and your relationships with others are a rich soil in which creativity can take root. Reflect on the memories that stand out most and see how you can use, and share with others, the feelings and thoughts that arise.

- **Other artists.** Sometimes the work of other artists can be an inspiration for us. This is perhaps particularly true when we are enjoying the creations of an artist who works in a different medium. Taking in the paintings at an art exhibit can inspire a poet's work. Listening to inspiring music can encourage a potter to create new designs.

- **Odd juxtapositions.** Sometimes we see, hear or experience something that seems incongruous to us and it can be of use to us in our creative work. They are often rich in metaphor. To quote lyrics from a song Quester wrote, 'Have you ever seen an eagle soar? Have you ever seen an eagle with its beak all covered in gore?' A more well-known example would be the image of a soldier holding a gun with a flower stuck in the barrel.

- **Meditation, prayer and magick.** Call on the divine in circle or get in touch with your muses and ask them to inspire your work. Allow your conscious mind to wander as you meditate, breathing deeply and watching the images or ideas arise.

- **Deadlines.** Sometimes having a time limit can help us to bring a project to a successful completion. Perhaps you need to finish a gift in time for a friend's birthday, submit a story for publication by a certain date or maybe you've a self-imposed deadline for completing a project. The pressure to finish your work can sometimes help you find just the right final touches.

Whatever your milieu, may you find the time, energy and inspiration to explore your natural creativity this fall season. Enjoy!

Mabon 2007: Storing the Harvest

Ah, Mabon! The harvest is in full swing, the beauty of nature evident everywhere. All around us, we can see fresh fruits and vegetables, planted with care in the spring and tended so carefully all summer. They are now ready to be brought in from the fields, orchards and gardens. At the same time, the sunlight has changed from the hot white of high summer to the golden hue of autumn. Twilight falls earlier and there is a chill in the air that wasn't there a few weeks ago. It is time, in the midst of all this bounty, to prepare for the winter to come.

For our ancestors, that meant the literal work of putting aside food for the colder months. Canning, drying and preserving the foods of the harvest was the main focus at this time of year. Everyone pitched in to make sure that enough food was safely stored away. These days, we can go to the supermarket and find what we need, even in the depths of winter. Yet we are still part of the Wheel of Life and the impulse to store away that which sustains us is a valid one.

In terms of our energies and projects, what is it that we are storing? If our work is tied to the seasons, we might put aside money in the bank for the winter months. As an artist or writer, we may set aside images and experiences that we enjoyed during the warm months, to inspire new creative projects. We may attend fall festivals, purchasing yarn or herbs that we'll set aside for our fall and winter creations.

This time of year is often busy and being outside more and staying more active can provide lots of good ideas that we may not have time to pursue. I keep a notebook close by and jot down inspirations to follow up on later. Part of the harvest might involve storing those thoughts, so that we can pull them out on long winter evenings and spin them into stories, spells or other creations. Save a list of such ideas on your computer or bulletin board, and you may be surprised what can be made with them.

Emotionally, it is important to be aware of what we are storing. We might have visited far-away family and friends this summer and want to keep the feelings of joy and fun to savor throughout the winter. When we send them a card or letter at Yule, we can bring to mind the fun times spent together at camp or on a trip. Yet if we've experienced loss or pain this year, we should be careful about not storing those feelings in the body. We may wish to save our grief for a letting-go ritual at Samhain, but suppressed emotions can do damage to both physical and mental health. Keep the memories, but let the feelings about them flow through, so that they can be released.

On a spiritual level, I find that it is easier this time of year to remember that all things are interconnected. Nature is flourishing and the earth is warm and welcoming. I like to save these images for those stark winter days when the plants and trees are bare of leaves and a cold wind whips across the fields. Snuggled in my warm home, I can flavor my meditations and visualizations with images of blooming flowers and singing birds. All of the seasons have their own beauty, and yet, like creating a savory sauce from a jar of our plump garden tomatoes on a cold winter's night, we can nourish ourselves with images of Mother Earth at her most colorful. May your harvest be bountiful and sustain you through the months to come. Blessed Be!

Mabon 2008: Choosing Love

When you're facing decisions that are difficult to make, experiencing events that you don't like or just feeling like your life isn't what you want it to be, it's easy to choose fear. Yet if you focus on lack, or what you don't want, that's exactly what you are drawing to you. Sympathetic magick is the most basic and important part of spellcasting and you may not even be aware you're doing it. Like resonates with like. Spending your time complaining only reinforces those things you aren't enjoying.

What if, instead, in each moment, you made a practice of choosing love, joy and harmony? I'm not talking about putting your head in the sand and pretending everything is just fine when you feel it's not. Rather, it's the deliberate choice to focus on the most positive action you can take, the most uplifting thought you can muster or the most joyful or pleasant feeling you can entertain *right now*.

The continued practice of choosing love brings you to a place of being in the moment and open to what it might bring. You may not be perfect at it right away, and everyone has a hard moment or a bad day once in a while. Yet if you do your best to find loving choices and thoughts and feelings, it will become a habit. You'll be more forgiving of yourself as well as others in your life. You'll feel your own power-from-within more strongly as you create change all around you.

The main challenge I have found with this practice is that you are only responsible for your own choices and attitudes. The people around you, even those you are closest to, are walking their own paths. As you change your attitudes and actions, they may not recognize it or they may be resistant to your new ways of being. They might even feel jealousy and resentment, or blame you for their own dissatisfaction and pain. It may be hard for them to see your joy. Simply be as kind as you can while remaining true to your own path.

Change of any type can be challenging and you may encounter your own resistance to it, falling back into old habits at odd moments or when you're under stress. You can create reminders for yourself, which let you know that it's okay to be afraid and yet still choose love. Whether they are Post-it notes on your mirror, your favorite incense wafting over your altar or special tattoos inscribed on your body, these reminders will be unique to you. Trust yourself and be kind as you negotiate this new way on your journey.

When you embark on the practice of choosing love, you'll know the way. Follow your feelings and intuitions, going with what feels really right to you, deep down, in each moment. Eating a hot fudge sundae with pure childlike joy is better for you than consuming a green salad with resentment and boredom. Do your best to harm none, including yourself, and then do as you will; your will backed up by the love that your spirit is made of. Follow your heart, and while I'm not promising that your life will be instantly easier, it can soon become more full, true and open to creativity and potential.

Don't let cynicism or coolness hold you back. Love isn't corny or weak. It's the most power-*full* force in the universe. Try it for a short time and see what unfolds. You might be surprised what you draw to you and how the external circumstances of your life change to suit your desires. And, rather than the energy of fear or anger or dissatisfaction, you'll be attracting more fun and kindness and love into your life while still learning new things each day. Why else be here?

Mabon 2009: Questions, Milestones and Pendulums

I sit down in a quiet consultation room with my chiropractor, who also acts as a nurturing spiritual counselor for those in her wellness practice. It's time for my yearly evaluation and she has a concerned look on her normally beaming face. 'You're in the midst of a deep transformation,' she tells me and describes the image that came to her: a pendulum. She shows me charts and pictures, demonstrating how I'm now at the still place at the bottom of the arc, awaiting motivation and fire, very like the place I was in four years ago. I have described an arc, from confident to despondent and back to bewildered. I clutch my

Kleenex, her words and energies resonating with the way I've been feeling over the past few months.

I left my 'day job' of many years in the spring of 2008 and I've not yet fully stepped into my new role. Tears well up again as she describes me as 'spread thin,' and suggests I focus on my goals and intentions, and becoming who I really am. I walk dazed through the rest of my day. It's clear that I've been here before and found my way out, but I can't remember how. I'm spread thin and constantly busy, but I'm not accomplishing anything tangible. I journal frantically, coming up with more questions than answers. My energy level seems lower than ever, my fire banked and faltering.

Quester's reaction to my account of the evaluation initially confuses me: he seems joyful on my behalf. 'That's great! You're poised to leap into your next new adventure!' BlackLion advises me to just do what brings me joy, though at the moment that means staying in bed with a book and a purring kitten or two. I ask myself, 'How did I get back to this stuck place so quickly? Why is the cycle so short? What am I doing wrong?' A dear friend turns it around, pointing out that I've traversed the spiral quickly, having successfully learned what I needed to learn.

The moon, waxing toward full, is amazing and I gaze up at her, letting my feelings and questions flow through my heart. 'What do I do next? Do I need more self-discipline? Should I create a daily schedule for myself? Be more aware of what I'm doing and when? Or do I simply change how I *feel* about what I'm doing in each moment? Be mindful no matter what is going on around me?' I return again and again to my yoga mat, using my practice to help center and ground my swirling thoughts.

By the end of the week, I'm feeling the crisper air of fall and the pull of the moon continues to uplift me. Rather than a morass to be stuck in, I'm starting to see my current situation as a foundation to push off from. My fire is awakening. I find I'm able to release some of my worries and insecurities: 'Is my writing good enough to publish? What should my creative focus be? Who will be interested in what I have to say? How will I make money?'

Taking a full day and night to relax and explore myself, I set an intention to release old patterns and encourage confident creativity. My positive focus surprises me; there really isn't much to release and my questions have now become inspiring rather than upsetting. Some doubts linger, but they aren't as pervasive as before. I find that I am, as my loved ones have suggested, set up to really shine on this next phase of my journey.

And so I tell myself: I'm surrounded by a vibrant community of people who want to hear what I have to share ('Really? They want to learn from me?'). The cookbook I co-authored is done and has been sent to four publishers. BlackLion and I are being offered more drumming gigs. And, while re-reading the intro-duction to a book we had drafted and then put aside a couple of years ago, I'm surprised by the high quality of the writing ('Did we really write this?!').

Our infrastructure is in place: we have a website, blogs and a network of friends and acquaintances online who share similar interests. Respected community members have offered us space to teach workshops and want us to work with them. Many in my network of friends are also working for themselves and are open to collaboration.

Who set all this up? Well, um...I did! With help, of course, and over many years of (sometimes hesitantly) speaking my truths and sharing my creativity. Ever since I can remember, I've wanted to be *older* than I am, to possess and embody the wisdom of a valued member of society, to have the knowledge and credi-bility to teach others. At last, it seems, I have arrived at a place where I begin anew to traverse the spiral, learning and growing as I journey onward. My milestone 40th birthday this month has opened up new channels of energy, bringing new confidence and affirming my callings. I can now say it and really believe it: I am a writer, a teacher, a drummer. I am a Pagan elder and my voice *is* being heard...and valued.

References

Aron, Elaine N., *The Highly Sensitive Person: How to Thrive When the World Overwhelms You* (Broadway Books, NY; 1996)

Byrne, Rhonda, *The Secret* (Atria Books, NY; 2006)

Carroll, Lewis, *Alice's Adventures in Wonderland* (Macmillan and Co., London; 1866)

Cunningham, Scott, *Living Wicca: A Further Guide for the Solitary Practitioner* (Llewellyn, St. Paul, MN; 2002)

Cunningham, Scott, *Sacred Sleep: Dreams & the Divine* (Crossing Press; 1992)

Dooley, Mike, *Notes From the Universe: New Perspectives from an Old Friend* (Atria Books, NY; 2003)

Grant, Richard, *Tex and Molly in the Afterlife* (Avon Books, NY; 1996)

Kabat-Zinn, Jon, *Wherever You Go There You Are: Mindfulness Meditation in Everyday Life* (Hyperion, NY; 1994)

Linn, Denise, *Sacred Space: Clearing and Enhancing the Energy of Your Home* (Ballantine Books, NY; 1995)

Ravenwolf, Silver, *To Stir a Magick Cauldron* (Llewellyn, St. Paul, MN; 1997)

Rinpoche, Sogyal, *The Tibetan Book of Living and Dying* (HarperCollins, NY; 1992)

Roberts, Jane, *Seth Speaks* (Prentice Hall, NJ; 1972)

Serith, Ceisiwr, *The Pagan Family: Handing the Old Ways Down* (Llewellyn, St. Paul, MN; 1995)

Simms, Maria Kay, *The Witch's Circle* (Llewellyn, St. Paul, MN; 1994)

Starhawk, *Dreaming the Dark* (Beacon Press, Boston, MA; 1982)

Starhawk and Valentine, Hilary, *The Twelve Wild Swans: A Journey to the Realm of Magic, Healing, and Action* (HarperCollins, San Francisco, CA; 2001)

Moon Books invites you to begin or deepen your encounter with Paganism, in all its rich, creative, flourishing forms.